The Law
The Lawyers
and
The Lawless

Beverley Stovell

Best Wishes

Dele

22/2/11

Dedicated
to
the memory of
my father,
a lawful man

Dele Ogun

The Law
The Lawyers
and
The Lawless

New European Publications
London 2009

Published in the United Kingdom in 2009 by
New European Publications
14-16 Carroun Road
London SW8 1JT, England

British Library Cataloguing in Publication Data

ISBN 978-1-872410-75-3
Copyright © 2009 by Dele Ogun
All rights reserved

Artwork and design: Mike Winter
Page Design: Luise Hemmer Pihl

Printed in England by
imprintdigital.net

ACKNOWLEDGMENTS

My thanks goes to the three wise old men of England, John Papworth, John Coleman and Sir Richard Body MP, who together gave me the encouragement to put pen to paper. My sympathies go to Chika Ene and Tamie Lewis who, between them, had the difficult task of typing up my carefree manuscripts. My appreciation goes to Helen Carroll and Luise Hemmer Pihl who, respectively, performed the arduous task of proof-reading and type-setting this work to apply the polish to my raw efforts. My love goes to my wife, Esther Ebelechukwu, whose vigilant watch on the work has held me within the bounds of the printable and whose enthusiasm has carried me through to the finish line. The last word is for my mother, Regina Aiyeyomi, who has been there at every staging post of the journey to date and who scraped and saved the money for the air-ticket for that first flight!

CONTENTS

You can discuss this book with Dele Ogun
at www.deleogun.com

1. OPENING SUBMISSIONS

On a date now forgotten in November, 1969, Master Akindele Ogunetimoju, then aged seven, was put on board a British Overseas Airways Corporation flight that was departing Lagos for London at 09.45 hours. He was headed for the English Bar though he did not know it.

From the Rainforest

My father, Emmanuel Akinlade Ogunetimoju, whom I knew not since he had left for England three months after my arrival in this world on 9 February, 1962, had made the decision from his home in Highbury, Islington. Between him and my mother, Regina Aiyeyomi Ogunetimoju, whom I remembered not, since she had left to join her husband when I was age one and three quarters, the plans had been made.

A year previously my father had directed that I be sent to Lagos from our village so that I could start learning English. Although Britain had granted Nigeria "independence" on 1 October, 1960, a year or so before my birth, the schools in the then capital city Lagos still observed the best of colonial traditions by requiring us children to make the transition out of the vernacular language, in which we were then thinking, to the English language, in order to receive our education. Liberal lashes of the cane awaited those who made the mistake of defaulting to their mother tongue.

At this stage of my life I knew nothing but my mother tongue, Yoruba, which I spoke in the Ikale dialect. As a Cornishman's English is to the ears of a Londoner so my Yoruba was to the people of Lagos. You see, although I had been born in Lagos, I had, on my mother's departure, been taken back to my father's village to live with my grandmother. There we had no need for another man's language to understand ourselves.

Aiyede (literal meaning 'life is here'), in the Osooro district of Ikale land, is a small village that sits on a plateau deep in the rainforest on the south west coast of Nigeria. My grandfather, Samuel Ogunetimoju, had been a man of standing at least by the generally low standards of the area. You could gauge this from the fact that the two-storey building which was his house competed with St. Andrew's Anglican Church as the tallest building in the village. Not that any of the villagers had a clue as to who this St. Andrew was especially as in moments of real extremis it was to Ogun (the Yoruba god of justice and war) that they still turned. The out-houses that stood immediately behind my grandfather's house were occupied by his several wives of which my grandmother was one.

Here then was the place where the lawyer who was later to be called to the English Bar, before becoming a corporate tax lawyer in the City and the first black lawyer to found and lead a commercial law firm in England, spent his formative years.

Only that at this stage he did not think of himself as black; much in the same way as his counterparts growing up in rural England did not think of themselves as white. Each was growing up in his own environment and so there was no basis for comparison. Yes, of course, we teased the children in the village who had lighter pigmentation by calling them "Oyinbo" (one whose face has been peeled by the wind), the nickname that adults used for white people, but none of us understood the true import of the word as we had never seen a white person.

Aiyede was a child's paradise. We were blind to the poverty that surrounded us and to the politics that gave rise to it. All we saw were the mangoes, bananas, water melons, pineapples, oranges, pears and coconuts that were all around us. Our playground was anywhere and everywhere: from the courtyard that lay between my grandfather's house and the church, to the trees and farms that surrounded the mud huts that made up the village.

Furniture being sparse and electricity being unheard of, our life was forever outdoors. Clothes were what we burdened ourselves with on Sundays only when we were going to church. For the rest

Me in Aiyede, with everything but the shoes

of the time underpants were all that we needed. We had no need for
toys either because, with a little improvisation, we made our own
out of whatever we could find. Occasionally a relative visiting from
Lagos might do us the kindness of bringing back a plastic ball, but
we were happy to make do with anything that we could kick and,
since the hot sun combined with the hard earth had made our feet
as hard as any football boots, there was quite a lot that we could
kick.

Our best pastime of all was the daily meetings at Lefun, nature's
very own bathing pool formed from the stream that snaked through
the rainforest at the bottom of the valley behind the church.
Downstream served as the village launderette and public bath,
while the waters upstream, purified, as they were, by the rocks and
thick foliage through which they oozed, provided pure drinking
water for the village.

The descent down the steep sides of the valley was long and hard.
The ascent was harder still because we would now be balancing
several litres of water on our heads in a variety of plastic vessels.
Only the knowledge that all the other kids in the 'hood would be
down by the stream made the journey tolerable.

Our diving boards were the low-lying branches of trees standing
on the banks of the stream. Only after you had tired yourself of
the water races and water fights would you ask one of the bigger
children to help you fill up your water container in the upstream
section where the water was deeper. Once they had done you the
further kindness of placing the water container on your head, the
long trek back up the valley side would begin.

To Lagos

This was the world that I knew until one morning, when I was 6, I
was woken by an uncle at the first crow of the cock at about 4:30
a.m. London time. He had come to carry out my father's instruction
that I should be taken to Lagos, the first staging post of my journey
to the English Bar. The operation had to be carried out before my
grandmother woke as otherwise it would not have been allowed to
happen. Thus, like a kidnapped slave, I was whisked out of the life
that I had known without opportunity to say farewell to my friends
and my grandmother. By the time the bells of the church sounded
the 5 a.m. alarm to summon the villagers to morning worship, we
were well on the way by motorbike: me, my uncle and the owner

of the motorbike.

At the Oniparaga junction of the motorway to Lagos we hitched a ride in the back of one of the open-top cargo lorries with wooden pallets that ply the road day and night. I remember being parceled up to the "conductor" like one of the items of cargo on which we sat before my uncle climbed aboard. At Ijebu-Ode we joined another vehicle to travel to Lagos in similar comfort. By adult calculations the journey was a mere 125 kilometeres or so but it felt like a journey without end through most of which I dozed.

The contrast between Lagos and the tranquility of Aiyede could not have been starker. The streets heaved with people and cars, while the air was filled with the babble of machines, man and other mammals. I did not like Lagos at all. The worst feature was the stench, especially in Isale Eko (downtown Lagos), where I was living with my uncle Mr Ojomo and his wife and three children: the twin boys Bode and Taiwo and their sister, Toyin.

Number 18 Omididun (literally "sweet water") Street could not have been more inappropriately named. The odour from the open gutters which ran through the corrugated shacks that served as homes was overwhelming. So much so that it wasn't long after my delivery into this hell-hole that I tried to find my own way back to Aiyede. I hadn't got very far when the attempt floundered at the bustling Tinubu Square roundabout. Not only did I not know which exit would take me to Aiyede, I now didn't know which exit would take me back to Omididun Street. Mercifully Lagos was then still a place where a run-away six-year-old could get lost and yet be found as a kind stranger took the tearful me to a policeman. At Moloney Police station I was reunited with my uncle and with Omididun Street.

A year later after some rudimentary schooling at ChristChurch Cathedral School on what was then Yakubu Gowon Street (now Broad Street), Lagos, to top up the even more rudimentary tuition from St Andrew's Primary School Aiyede, it was time for me to be torn again from the new crop of friends I had acquired in Lagos and be moved to the next staging post in my journey to the English Bar.

To Highbury & Islington
A place had been reserved for me at Drayton Park Primary School in Highbury, Islington. I had originally been booked to travel to

London on 4 October, 1969 but the British immigration authorities had not yet issued the entry certificate that would make my entry lawful. Finally, on 4 November, 1969, my father received a letter from one Mr S R Gibson of the British High Commission Immigration Department in the following terms:

"I now enclose the documents you sent us in connection with Akindele's entry certificate application. An entry certificate was issued on 29th October."

My entry having been legalized, I flew in as an unaccompanied minor, aged seven, on that date now forgotten in November, 1969, never having seen a plane before and with no understanding of the concept of flight. Looking back now, it was a feat almost as remarkable as Neil Armstrong's flight to the moon earlier in the same year.

The white female air-hostess, who was my handler, did her best to reassure me knowing full well that I understood precious little of her language, especially the way that she spoke it. Suddenly the plane came down with what to me felt like a very hard bump indeed. My instant panic was only assuaged by the applause and cries of "Praise God" coming from the other passengers. I had arrived in London, England.

As I gazed out of the window on this November evening the thing that struck me was the lights. I had never seen so much light when the sky was dark. I had also never seen so many white people. So this was the "ilu Oyinbo" (land of the white people) where, I had been told, my parents lived.

I had no idea what my parents looked like although my uncle had put a photo of my mother in the pocket of my suit to help me find her. In Yoruba culture a male child would not greet his parents by a hug and a kiss but by falling prostrate on the ground before them as you would if you were doing press ups (a female child would kneel). As I was being paraded by the air hostess along the Arrivals barrier, I prostrated at the feet of the first black man that I saw thinking him to be my father. Thankfully my blind search was cut short by a woman, who eventually turned out to be my mother. She had recognised the shaven-headed boy, in a black suit with his a little-brown suitcase, that she had left in Aiyede aged one-and-a-bit.

It was an uncle, not my father, who accompanied my mother to Heathrow airport that day. Dad was not the type for the emotion of an airport welcome for his first child, and only son, that he had not set eyes on since shortly after his birth. Eventually we arrived at the terrassed house in Highbury that my father, on his modest earnings from his civil service job and with the aid of a mortgage, had managed to buy for £4,000. This was a time long before the English themselves acquired the now incurable addiction for owning their own homes.

Number 50 Framfield Road was an end-of-terrace house with four rooms, kitchen and attic. My parents occupied the front room on the ground floor and rented the rest out as bedsits. It was the only way they could afford the mortgage. From the few photographs that I had seen of my father, I knew that he had once been a dapper dresser, complete with cravats, bowler hats and "walking-stick umbrellas". However, the realities of life as an immigrant in England appeared to have killed the dreams that he had been sold as a child of Empire. His wardrobe was now very functional.

It wasn't just him I was meeting for the first time as I also by then had two sisters, Femi and Kemi. The meeting with them was brief because they did not stay with my parents but with a retired English couple, Mr and Mrs Butler, in Woolwich, Charlton. This was an arrangement born of financial necessity because both hands, Mum's and Dad's, were needed on deck to service the mortgage. Thus the Ogunetimoju family of London lived together as a family for one weekend in every other month. In the intermediate month we would take the train to Charlton to pay the Butlers and my sisters a Sunday visit. This was a trip that I always looked forward to because I liked the Butlers. I liked Frank Butler because he used to play professional football with Charlton Athletic F.C. I liked Mrs Butler because she baked very nice rock cakes.

The two girls, having lived with the Butlers virtually since birth, had been raised as proper little madams with proper English diction who had their hair in rollers each night. Though of the same blood, coming as we did from such radically different backgrounds we were on course for culture wars from the beginning. They found everything I said funny because of my accent and poor English. For my part I found them as trying as they were charming because they were fond of telling me, their Egbon (their senior), to "stop being silly", which was pure sacrilege where I was coming from. They remained with the Butlers until Femi turned seven, when they were brought home to join me at Drayton Park School. By this time Remi, the youngest girl, had arrived.

Drayton Park Primary School was a short walk from our house. I settled into the school quickly for two reasons: I was a very good footballer and a pretty good fighter. For these reasons the initial teasing over my accent did not last very long. Besides, with my father insisting on communicating with me only in English, and with the extra lessons that I received at lunch time with the more educationally challenged children, it didn't take that long for me to reach the stage where I could hardly speak Yoruba anymore. In any event, in these early years in England my longing was to belong and not to be the odd one out. Since my sisters didn't understand Yoruba and no one at school appeared to be interested in it, there seemed to me to be no point in continuing with this museum language that only my mother seemed to have a passion for.

My new life in Britain was bitter-sweet. On the one hand I was now with my family, in a land where they had light, water and toilets that you could sit on; on the other hand I was swopping the carefree abandon of life in a village in Nigeria to be holed up in a crowded house in England with an education-obsessed disciplinarian of a father.

The routine quickly became settled. From the moment he arrived from his civil service post in Whitehall at about 6p.m., the instruction would be "Go and take your book". We would study, English and Maths alternately until 8.30p.m., when we broke for supper and the BBC's Nine O'clock News. The routine was made harder by the knowledge that all my schoolmates in the neighbourhood were out playing football or watching children's programmes like Scooby Doo and The Harlem Globetrotters. It was small wonder that I had little to contribute to playground discussions about what was on TV the night before especially as world affairs never really came up in the discussions.

Saturday was my official day off from studies because, as my father was fond of saying, "All work and no play makes Jack a dull boy". English idioms and idiomatic expressions were my father's love. Sunday morning was church followed by football up to 6p.m. when I would again be instructed to go and take my book.

While other children loved and looked forward to school holidays, I hated them. Holiday camp for me was Islington Central Library on the Holloway Road. My father dropped me off there in the morning on his way to the office and collected me back in the evening on his way home. I must have read virtually all the books in the children's library. I stacked the books high on my table, in much the same way as the King's advisers stacked the Princess's mattresses in the tale of the Princess and the Pea.

With school holidays spent in such solitude and seriousness, I grew to love school because at least we had lots of play time. As I grew older and bolder during these primary school years, I sometimes sneaked out of the library to go and play in Highbury fields. Still I had to be careful because my mother worked in the local laundry and she sometimes dropped in on me with some cake or sweets. Luckily, my involuntary minders, the librarians, never squealed on me. I take this opportunity to thank them.

Thus it was that my childhood years in London were characterised by stolen moments of freedom and pleasure in between hours of study under the vigilant watch of my parents. Knowing that if I asked to be allowed to go out and play football after school I would be refused, I would arrange for one or another of my friends in the 'hood to pop the question. They knew exactly when to come calling because my father would invariably have to walk past them on his way from Drayton Park Station. The request would be granted no more than twice in a week and on the strict condition that I was to be back within one hour. Woe betide you if you were ever late back and so it did betide me on one particular occasion.

Football was my passion and, during these hard times, my only joy. The match that night, against some boys from the Addington Mansions Estate in Highbury Barn, must have been especially enthralling because I completely lost track of time. The recently installed floodlights at Highbury Fields helped to disguise that night had fallen. It was around 8p.m. when my team mates drew my attention to the figure of my mother standing at the perimeter fence. Like an escaped convict at the moment of recapture, my high crashed into an instant low because I knew what I was in for and, from what she said, Mum knew it too.

I received the full complement of twenty-four lashes from my father's whip (a doubled-up electrical flex) that night without interruption. He had taken the precaution of locking the two of us into the room from the inside so that none of the tenants who my anguished cries had alarmed could interfere with the judge's sentence.

My father was not a wicked man. He was simply anxious for

my future. He had been raised in a harsh environment where the approach to education was unapologetically Dickensian: the lubricant for all education was the cane. He often amused us with stories from his own childhood in colonial Nigeria when teachers would sadistically dole out twenty-four and thirty-six lashes of the cane for minor misdemeanors. His ambition for me was driven by the career frustrations that he had experienced and was experiencing. His academic ability lay well beyond his qualifications and the lowly civil service post that he had managed to secure. Whilst working as a file-carrying administrative officer by day, at night he would be reading his law books while taking time out to teach me algebra and the characteristics of "past participles" in English grammar.

Well at least he did his best to invest me with this learning, because I was not a model student. Neither he nor I, at this stage, understood how my mind worked, but the manifestations brought us to the same conclusion (though we did not voice it to each other) that I was not bright at all. The evidence was that I could never remember the simplest instructions; it was as if my brain dumped all information that it came into contact with at the very instant of contact.

Given what he knew of his own academic capabilities, and with my mother having been headmistress of St. Andrew's primary school in Aiyede, he put my apparent slowness down to lack of concentration the only remedy for which was liberal application of the whip. He had never heard of dyslexia and neither had I. My predicament was compounded by the fact that I was especially slow at maths, a subject for which he had special aptitude. As a result, it was with dread that I would approach his table with my supposed answers to the assignments that he had set for me.

Despite his and my best efforts, I didn't get the 11+ results that would have got me into Central Foundation, the grammar school that he had in mind. I went instead to Highbury Grove Boys School, the local comprehensive. I was secretly delighted because this was where most of my friends were going.

Highbury Grove at that time had an excellent headmaster, Dr Rhodes Boyson, who left the school to become a Member of Parliament. He was later to become Minister for Education for the Conservative Party under Margaret Thatcher. While the headmaster could make a claim to excellence, the boys at the school could not. We really were a very mixed bunch in the best of comprehensive school traditions.

I redeemed myself a little in my father's eyes by passing six out of my seven O Levels with good grades. The shine was taken off because I got a D in maths. I re-sat my maths O Level during the first year of the sixth form and scraped up to a C grade – to think that I then ended up as a tax lawyer! In the sixth form, I started out doing four A Levels: history, economics, government & politics and English literature.

Talk of university came quite early after my O Levels. For me, with no antecedents to follow, this next level had as much appeal as a journey to an unknown planet for the unadventurous. Neither of my parents had been to university and those remoter members of my family who had were far away in Nigeria.

A Levels had been foreboding enough and my feeling was that degrees were for the very bright and the evidence showed that I was clearly not that kind of scholar. Since, at that time, I had a great dread of looking foolish in public, and having become aware that I was the only one in my year taking four A Levels, I resolved to drop one. But how was I going to explain it to my father?

I spun him a yarn that the teachers had pointed out to me that I was the only one taking four A Levels and they had warned me that it could be too much when the exams came round. He was always one to believe whatever the teachers said and so the trick worked. Which one to drop was a tough decision because I was good at all. In the end I decided to let English go since I was a little weak on English poetry, (the Milton and Yeats type etc, not the Chaucer and Alexander Pope style).

Thus it was that after the first year of the A Levels I jettisoned English literature for fear of being picked out at university as being clever. How was I to know that some at the English Bar would have more A Levels than I had O Levels. To compound matters the grades that I got in my remaining A Levels were disappointing: history C; government & politics C; economics D. The disappointment was made worse by the realisation that it was Chaucer's *The Pilgrim's Tale* that came up in the A Level English literature exam that I had dropped.

It was scant consolation for me that out of all those who took the A Level history exam at Highbury Grove that year I was the only one who passed, albeit with a C grade. Up until this point the only award that I had ever received at the annual school prize-giving-night was the 100 percent attendance certificate which I unfailingly collected every year. In the contest between going to school and staying at home, there was only ever one winner for me. Now, however, I was the undisputed champion in history at Highbury Grove for 1980. I had put in a lot of effort in preparing for the exams – my father ensured that I did and I had in any event imbibed the habit of devoting myself to my studies.

My Old Man

Emmanuel Akinlade Ogunetimoju was of that class of Nigerians who came to the U.K. in the early 1960s from the newly independent Nigeria with one purpose in mind: to graduate and return home to take up the opportunities being vacated by the British colonial masters. He was of the group that would work 9-5 Monday to Friday in Her Majesty's Civil Service (private sector jobs were out of the question then) and then spend the whole of Saturday in a public library, studying for his A Levels in law and government & politics by correspondence. Wolsey Hall College study manuals were ever present in our house.

A master of the English language and grammar and a craftsman with the pen, he had more of the standard aptitudes for law than I did. However, the closest that he would eventually get to his dream was when, towards the end of his working life, he worked as a member of the court staff at the Royal Courts of Justice in the Strand. The consolation for him was to make me into a lawyer instead.

Not that this was an easy thing to do because I have never been a conformist. If something was not me I would never gladly suffer it. Thus having made up my mind by the age of eleven that the Church was not for me, I bided my time until I turned sixteen to make a unilateral declaration of independence in matters religious. For my father who was a regular at Christ Church Highbury, and more so for my mother whose father had been an ordained priest in the Anglican faith, it was a great shock.

As a teenager I, actually, did not know what a lawyer did. I had never met one and my father never explained to me why I should be a lawyer let alone why he thought I would be any good at it. All I knew was that whenever any of his friends asked me what I wanted to be, he would always volunteer the answer, "He is going to be a lawyer". It was much later that I came to understand that for most Africans of his generation if your child was not a doctor, an accountant, an engineer, an architect or a lawyer, he was a failure. So it was that many who would have achieved great fame and success as sportsmen and entertainers were led astray.

My father's careers counseling was ever-remarkable for its simplicity. Kemi, my sister, having shown an early aptitude for science subjects and maths, he wasted no time in slating her down to become a doctor. For her protest that she couldn't bear the sight of blood he had a simple solution. He went to Petticoat Lane Market and bought a dozen or so live chickens to slaughter. He reckoned that by the time she had learnt to slaughter all of them her phobia for blood would have been cured.

My preparation for my assigned career was, mercifully, less gory. It involved watching the TV drama Crown Court. While I found the programme enthralling, it all but convinced me that I could never be a barrister because the one skill that I could see that you needed was the ability to address an audience. At this stage of my life there was nothing that I was more hopeless at.

The very thought of it filled me with dread. I had scored an F grade on my O Level oral English exam – the only person who failed the exam that it was said could not be failed. The exam entailed my sitting in a room with four of my colleagues from the O Level English class and discussing the concept of "canned laughter". The question didn't allow for the fact that I came from a household where I was only allowed to watch football, wrestling and the Nine O'clock News. From there the discussion moved on to Ancient Rome where again I found myself handicapped by the fact that I had somehow not been selected to do Latin even though I found languages very easy. By the time the discussion got to a topic on which I could contribute, I could not find an easy point of entry since all had been convinced by this time that I had been struck dumb. Having failed to contribute a single word to the discussion, the only grade I could have been given was an F.

But the signs of the problems that I had with speaking in public had been present all through our regular English classes. Whenever we were allocated passages to read out, our English teacher would mercifully give me the one-liners. Even then a million butterflies would suddenly manifest themselves in my stomach as soon as I felt that my name was about to be called to read out aloud. My throat would constrict and my mouth would become dry as all the moisture would have been assigned by my brain to the sweat glands in my body.

Given this condition (which I now understand to be "social phobia"), as far as I was concerned my father was in dreamland whenever he announced, as he so often did, that I was going to be a lawyer. Instead, I made a secret resolution to study economics or sociology. Not that I knew what an economist or sociologist did; it was sufficient that I believed that they didn't have to speak in public.

In the end my reconciliation with my father's desire for me to become a lawyer came through a process of elimination. I was useless at science and weak on maths. My strengths were finding meaning in words used, whether Medieval English or modern languages, analyzing and understanding events that had happened, and I could write quite well. With no real insight into the alternatives that might have been available to me with this mix of strengths and weaknesses, reading law had the attraction that those who read law became lawyers such that I would not have to worry about what to do once I had finished. Having made peace with myself and with my father over the next stage of my journey to the English Bar, I used the prize-money vouchers from my A Level history prize to buy some books, one of which was *The Speechmaker* by Granville Janner QC MP. After all I still had this serious handicap to overcome.

The A Level grades that I had got meant that I couldn't take up any of the offers that I had received to study law at School of Oriental and African Studies, London School of Economics or Queen Mary College. I had restricted my applications to the London universities because I could not afford to live away from home even with a full grant. I had to be where the casual jobs were that would tide me through. Besides I had never been outside of London since my arrival.

My first "Holiday"

I decided to take a year off to work to raise the money I needed for my first "holiday" back to Nigeria and also to repeat my A Level Economics in the meantime. The homecoming was an emotional experience for me; despite the dust, I felt the urge to embrace the soil of Mother Africa with a kiss as we disembarked. I was staying with my uncle, Mr Segun Akinmosin (he was a blood relative somewhere down the line although in Nigeria every relative, friend or acquaintance of one's parents of an appropriate age is an "uncle" or "aunty") and his family in Anthony Village. He was the Director of Administration at Nigerian Merchant Bank and gave me my first insight into how high one could fly in one's own country. There were so many other uncles and aunties that my father had said that I had to see, not that I actually knew any of them.

He didn't need to tell me to go to Aiyede as it had never left my mind. It was another, more senior uncle, Dr. Ijose, who had claimed the glory of leading the procession for my return to the village where my story had really begun. On seeing me, my grandmother declared that she was now ready to die and needed some persuasion to stay a while longer.

As I sat on a stool outside the same old outhouse with the same old corrugated roofing, which was her house, I heard a terrifying sound that I had not heard since I left. The early warnings were the sound of children screaming as they made their frantic escape. Then I heard the rustle of the long grass that formed part of its attire. I sensed it was coming in my direction as the jangling bells and cowrie shells on its feet increased in intensity with my heartbeat. Suddenly it appeared from around the corner: it was a masquerade (a returnee from the spirit world according to African folklore). With its face covered and a big stick in hand, I froze as it came towards me. Then in a muffled growl it said my name:

"Akindele ni yi! (literally this is Akindele)

Now a masquerade is not supposed to speak the language of humans but I was mightily relieved that this one did and that he knew me.

On my return, I applied for jobs with the A Levels that I had but couldn't get any. With hindsight the private sector jobs weren't forthcoming because of my name; as to this more will be told later. I could not get the public sector jobs at the Higher Executive Officer level because I couldn't get past the non-verbal reasoning tests that featured consistently in the selection process. In truth, I couldn't even understand the examples in the test papers. Thus I would sit through the whole test trying to make sense of the pictures and images before me while the other candidates were flying through them. The fact is that I had never seen non-verbal reasoning tests before; we certainly didn't have them at Highbury Grove. My feeling of inadequacy for the world of work was increasing.

In the circumstances I had no choice but to drop my aspirations to the level of clerical officer which is an O Level standard. I ended up in the tax office at Edmonton Green as a Tax Officer. I now had my father's life style: by day I worked as a junior civil servant, by night I studied for my A Level Economics retake. I eventually scraped a more respectable C grade.

Now equipped with my three C grades at A Level, the only place I could have read law in London was at one of the then polytechnics. That I chose the Polytechnic of North London had less to do with the fact that the law precinct was just up the road from Highbury Grove School and more to do with one of my father's tenants.

We had moved from 50 Framfield Road not long after I had started at Highbury Grove. The circumstances of the move still registers as one of the greatest shocks that I have experienced. I returned from school one day in the company of some of my school mates to see a signboard in the front yard of the house: "SOLD".

"Akindele, are you moving?" my friend asked.

"I guess so", was my absent-minded reply.

No one had told me what was in the offing. There had been no "FOR SALE" sign because, as it turned out, it was Islington Council that had simply issued a compulsory purchase order in respect of the house. Looking back now there was no justification for their action as the house was in good condition and was well maintained. Further, the house has reverted back to private ownership now that it lies in the shadow of Arsenal's Emirates Stadium.

Having been thus uprooted, my parents had bought a new and larger house on the other side of Highbury Grove School, at No. 43 Pyrland Road. Again tenants were ever present in the house but at least, in this larger house, there was a better divide between the family quarters and the tenanted areas.

The Roads Begin To Part

One such tenant, Niyi Agbaje, was reading Business Studies at the Polytechnic of North London which has since, through a series of mergers, become London Metropolitan University. He was the resident D.J. for their International Black Students' Society and he had invited me to one of their dances. When I saw the babes at that dance and heard the music, I knew that this place had more appeal for me than the clever-looking people at the other universities I had visited.

Subconsciously I was impressed by the fact that there were so many black students there. It was so much closer to the ethnic mix that I had been used to at primary and more so at secondary school.

I guess that I was still in search of that anonymity that I had left behind in Nigeria where I did not stand out. Music was the biggest influence on my life at this stage and that dance determined that I was going to do my law degree at London Metropolitan University. It was to prove a fortuitous decision.

Since familiarity always breeds complacency, knowing that the law campus, at Ladbroke House, was only 200 yards further up from Highbury Grove School, I arrived a little late on the day of enrolment. By the time I arrived all the students were in the full swing of introductions and opinionated discussions. My mind flashed back to my Oral English exam. It wasn't looking anything like that carefree dance where the "brothers" and "sisters" had been grinding and winding on the dance floor. Where were all those black students that I saw that night? There were only a few of them on the law course.

The loudest of them was Kevin McCourt. His loudness came not from his speech but from his laugh which was infectious for being uninhibited. His mother, whom he cherished, was a black Kenyan from the Kikuyu tribe. His father, who he seemed less fond of, had been a white Scot. Kevin was a mixed-race black nationalist with emerald green eyes. He was the most politically aware of us all. He had already struck up a close rapport with Comfort Ndumiso Mamba.

Comfort was from the Kingdom of Swaziland on the southern tip of the continent of Africa. His father was the High Commissioner to London for the Kingdom. Comfort was defined by his clothes which, at a little over six foot, he carried well. In this regard he was almost the antithesis of Kevin. What they had in common was a good grasp of contemporary African political issues which they discussed at length. They never found consensus because Kevin was of a revolutionary bent while Comfort was a member of the royal court of one of the last remaining absolute monarchies in the world.

Being only a few years older than his friend, the Prince Regent of his country, Comfort was sorted career-wise even before he graduated. When the young Mswati III succeeded to his father's throne in 1986, Comfort effectively became legal adviser to the King and by virtue thereof to the Kingdom. The legality of the custom whereby the King chooses a new wife each year from a parade of bare-breasted female virgins (he is now on his fourteenth wife) is one that I know that my friend will defend to the last.

The political triad was completed by Peter Gwamanda, an ANC exile from South Africa. From him I got to know a little more about Nelson Mandela and Apartheid because the political discussions over lunch were always going over my head.

Thanks to the curriculum that we had followed in England, I knew a lot about the wonderful things that Lord Palmerston and his type were doing in Britain but nothing at all of the horrible things they had been doing in my homeland and in Africa generally. As a result of this selective tuition, names like Kwame Nkrumah, Patrice Lumumba and Walter Sisulu that were being bandied about in the discussions between Messrs McCourt, Mamba and Gwamanda meant little to me even though I had won the A Level history prize at Highbury Grove School. My contribution was like that of the umpire at a Wimbledon tennis match paying each participant equal attention without prejudice.

The discourse of the fourth black male, Peter Parkin, was much closer to what I had been accustomed to in young black male conversation in England. Peter was a very handsome, almost pretty, Jamaican in the mould of the pop star Prince. Like me he knew no politics and, unlike me, he had no interest. He would rather talk about music and babes and shoot pool.

I am not sure that I really met any of the white students on that first day though there were many of them. This was odd given that through virtually all of my secondary school years, I had tended to be the sole black representative in the O and A Level classes. In truth, at this stage of my life, I had started to beat the retreat back into my own community. I was now more conscious of the other sex and my taste was unequivocally black. As I used to say to anyone who cared to enquire, I preferred my chicken roasted.

Our taste in music had also begun to restore the natural divide. This was the late '70s and early '80s; the beginning of the phenomenon known as '80s Soul. On my side of the divide was the music you can only hear properly by feeling the rhythms. On this side were Shalamar's *Second Time Around,* Dynasty's *Do Me Right,* Chaka Khan's *Ain't Nobody* etc. On the other side of the divide were The Boomtown Rats' *I Don't Like Mondays,* Dexter's Midnight Runners' *Come On Eileen* and Madness' *Our House:* music that you heard but which you did not feel; songs that you sang along to rather than gyrated to. The roads of race, culture and destiny had definitely begun to part.

But the signs of the parting of ways socially were already there. The first sign was when it was suggested that we go for a drink after our final A Level exam. We trooped down to the Alwynn Castle on St. Paul's Road. Having never been in a pub before, the safest tactic was to join the herd and so I ordered "A pint as well". I almost spat the stuff out at the first taste. It was not for me and so I requested a Coke instead. I had fallen at the first hurdle of social integration as a young adult; for what is an Englishman's social life without alcohol? All the others stood there with pints in their hands exchanging stories. That was my first and last time in a pub until I got to Bar School. ▨

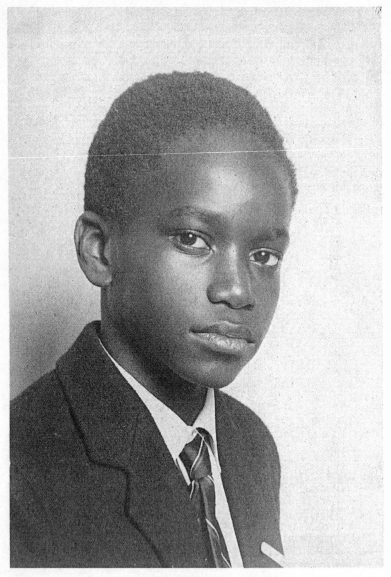

Me at Highbury Grove, the School Monitor

2. RHYTHM & REASON

At this stage of my life there were not many Nigerians in England. Oil was selling at over $40 a barrel and Nigeria produced over two million barrels a day of the stuff. The Naira (Nigeria's currency) was almost at par with the pound while Americans had to give up two of their dollars to get one of our Naira.

With good opportunities waiting at home, Nigerians came to the U.K. with clearly defined exit strategies. They came to do their degrees and as soon as they graduated they were on the plane home to secure the expected returns on the time invested. Those who were already collecting the dividends from their years of study and training came only for holidays and to do their shopping. It was a sight to see shops in the West End falling over themselves to welcome my people with:

"Would Sir like a cup of tea while he is waiting?"

The stores on Tottenham Court Road selling electronic equipment had bill boards outside promising "Tax Free Exports to Lagos" and declaring "Naira accepted here". The only Nigerians who stayed in England were those like us trapped in the poverty of opportunity because our parents had not yet completed their degrees. This was a mixed fortune for me because the poverty of opportunity for educational advancement in Nigeria for those like me with dyslexic minds is such that I would never have got to study law at all. That was the preserve of those with the most conventional of brains.

In the absence of my own people the black community that I found myself retreating into was the surrogate one of the West

Indian community. Trevor Williams, from Antigua, was my best friend then. We had been to the same primary and secondary schools, and we found that we shared the same interest in tennis, football, music and babes.

As for the last he always got the pick of the crop due to his "red skin" (the result of historic miscegenation) while I was pure black. This proved to be a bit of a handicap in the circles that I was mixing in since Caribbean parties and night clubs tend to be conducted in near pitch darkness as the men and women are, generally, too self-conscious to dance with the lights on. They were also remarkable for the fact that the room always fills up from the side walls as if there is a taboo on the centre until the hall is jam-packed and there is nowhere else to stand. This was a stark contrast to Nigerian parties where the rush is to be centre stage and ideally to have the dance floor all to yourself with the spotlight on your attire and your moves.

As a pure black, "pulling a dance" with the finest babes at such events was often a challenge, the courtship being conducted in silence by gently pulling on the elbow of the babe you want to dance with. There was one jam-packed session at the All Nations Club in Hackney when I tried pulling a dance only to discover that the person whose elbow I was gently pulling on was a man.

"Wha you want?" He turned and asked before shuffling away somewhat hurriedly.

Having inherited dance genes from my mother which needed room and lights for full expression, the Caribbean party formula was very much a compromise. The consolation was that when you did manage to pull a dance with someone (of the right sex!), their women are the best in the world in taking you to the edge, right there on the dance floor, as the lower parts become locked in perfect rhythm in a slow wind and grind. It was in fact the "slow grind" that also explained why the West Indian men rushed for the walls of the room or hall rather than the centre stage and why the parties were conducted in near darkness.

The love of music and dancing that Trevor and I shared led me to suggest that we form a D.J. outfit or a "Sound" as it was called in those days: after all we were spending so much on records. This was to be my first business venture. Bass 69, as our Sound was called, started with birthday party engagements but we quickly graduated to playing at college and university African-Caribbean Society dances. The high point was when we started booking dance halls in our own right and promoting the dances. The maiden promotion at the Horseshoe Theatre on London's Tottenham Court Road made us a profit of close to a £1,000 on that first night.

The best Sounds at that time were Roxy and Soul II Soul. They set the standard to which we aspired with top-ticket gigs in mega-dance halls that sold out as soon as the event was announced. Though Bass 69 played fantastic music, operating as we were without a "mike man" to "chat" on the mike, a Sound playing to a largely West Indian audience had no hope of making it really big.

The third member of our crew, Tunde, was not a "mike man". In truth he was not a music man at all. We brought him in because we needed the monetary contribution he could make towards the cost of the Citronic System 80 twin-deck sound-system that we needed to buy. It was an early lesson in how not to choose business partners. Having accepted his investment we needed to give him a sense of involvement and so I would get him to play first in the period when the audience were just arriving. Trevor would take over from him to start the dance off before I came on to the turntables to really turn the party on. Though we took great care to hide the fact that Tunde was not a music man by writing down the records that he should play and the sequence in which he should play them, we couldn't stop him giving the game away by repeatedly playing a 45 disc at a 33 or vice versa and then not realizing the error before the audience latched on.

Despite this handicap, we were a favorite at the International Black Students Society at London Metropolitan University so I earned a little bit of a reputation as the sound man and the dancer. I would later put my D.J. skills aside to focus on my law studies while Soul II Soul would go on to become the internationally acclaimed band and record label that produced the soul anthems "Back to Life" and "Keep on Moving". As it turned out the Sound was led by a contemporary of mine from the neighboring Holloway School who would become famous as the recording artist Jazzie B. Our paths would cross again later when I would be acting for Jazzie B as one of his legal advisers.

The parting of ways with my adopted English culture had been completed by another holiday that I had decided to take to Nigeria just before my degree course started. The hottest nightspot in Lagos then was Phase II Nite Club that a cousin had taken me to; and what a club it was. The club rules made it obligatory for a man to "excuse-me-dance" from the ladies with the quid pro quo being that the ladies were generally gracious in their response. It was a far cry from London. And, man were the ladies fine and the music hot! My resolve became like my father's, to finish my studies and head back home.

Getting to know me

The law degree did not start well for me. The introductory topics were largely airy-fairy discussions about the concept of society and the role of law within it. Everyone had an opinion which they were only to eager to voice; everyone that is except for me à la oral English O Level.

To my relief and joy, things changed when we started dealing with substantive legal issues. All of a sudden I felt the calling. I was in my element; I had found myself at last. law was, after all, the subject I was born for.

I found a rhythm in the subject with the same effortlessness with which I discerned the rhythm in my music and I felt the same confidence in stepping out as I did when on the dance floor. There was an immediate transformation in my character. The quiet man became the most vocal; the student who had always doubted his intellect became the most assured; the one who rarely had a viewpoint was now the most opinionated. The lecturer would barely have finished posing the problem before I was ready with the answer. What is more, I developed a knack for developing derivative reasoning from the illustrations and precedents given.

While many students were content to rely on the case summaries, I would settle for nothing less than the full law report and, most times, I would read all the judgments, concurring and dissenting as I went along. Having made books my friends from my early years and having made Islington library my second home, I felt a sense of ownership of the University law library as if it were my personal collection; I felt destined to make a name in the law.

By the end of the first term of the first year of the degree, I had acquired a reputation as a sharp legal mind. Shaun Wallace, a Caribbean student in the year above had become particularly fond of me for this reason. He would later become the first black person to win the BBC's *Mastermind of Great Britain* quiz challenge. If Shaun had said to any of us at the time that he was even going to enter the competition we would have all been rolling over with laughter but then the joke would have been on us. The point is that none of us appreciated how his mind worked. All we saw was the outer Shaun, a brilliant footballer who had been a bag of trouble in his youth and who had struggled, academically, to get to where he was. The only clue as to what lay beneath the bonnet was his rapid – fire wit. He could cuss like no other.

Coursework on substantive law issues rarely came back without an A grade (which I would signify to Shaun with a thumbs–up, on the occasions that he would peer enquiringly through the glass panel on the door to the tutorial room). Yet when the exams came round my grades were disappointing, just as my O and A levels had been. I consoled myself with the fact that the first year grades did not count towards the degree. I considered that only a first class would do me justice and an upper-second class was the minimum that I could accept. Such was my determination that I got to work during the summer holidays before the start of the second year of the degree. A girlfriend who was in her final year had given me her copy of Riddall: *Introduction to Land Law*. By the end of the summer I had understood all the concepts, "the rule against perpetuities" etc.

In that second year we studied land law, contract and tort with a non-law option which, for me, was Economics. I cruised through the tuition and coursework assignments and read hard for the exams. When the results came out I was anguished: A 2:1 in Economics and Contract; a 2:2 in Tort and a 3rd in Land Law. The 2:2 in Tort I put down to differences with the female lecturer who preferred a sociological approach to Tort to black letter analysis. But what could explain the 3rd in Land Law, my favourite subject in which I scored As on all coursework and in which I had read so many cases!

The results really knocked me back. The others in my year who were expected to get a minimum of a 2:1 degree had all performed to expectations and collected three or four 2:1 grades towards the aggregate of five out of nine that they needed over the second and final year. The performance set me thinking and my colleagues doubting. Would I make the 2:1 minimum that I felt I had to get to stand any chance of being the kind of lawyer that I felt that I could be?

I began a post-mortem of my exam technique. Why was it that in tutorials and coursework assignments I was top-flight but found it consistently hard to produce the same standard in exams? It occurred to me that the same problem had plagued my O Levels and A Levels: I always prepared diligently but the exam performance would always be well below the level of understanding of the subject that I had shown in the classroom.

The answer came to me, ironically, in the run-up to the second year exam but at a time when it was too late to affect my performance for that year. It came in the course of a group revision exercise to which I had been invited. Group revision exercises normally did not appeal to me as I found that the group generally moved at the pace of the person with the least understanding and, since understanding concepts was my strength, I derived no benefit from them. Indeed it was because of my understanding and ability to explain the concepts to others that I was invited. I attended this one because of the persistence of the friend who was organising it and because the venue was a few houses down from mine.

In the course of the exercise I was asked to explain a particular case. I found that I dried up in my recital of the facts of this very important case very quickly. I knew the principle that it established but I could not remember the key facts. A fellow student who I had explained the decision in the case to on an earlier occasion, took over from me and gave a comprehensive account of the salient facts.

There and then the handicap that I had been labouring under throughout my education became apparent. Yes, I could understand concepts better and faster than my counterparts but even those who needed my help to understand the concepts had a better and faster recall of the detail. I tested the thesis for my underperformance with memory tests and realized that my brain simply refused to store and retrieve pure data. The final confirmation came through a new friend, Dele Martins.

We met at Clissold Park while I was playing football with my friends from secondary school. He had come to the park with his cousin looking for a game. As the only black guy playing, they approached me to ask if they could join us. This is the joy of park football in that total strangers could gel as a team in an instant and great friendships can be made.

After the game, Dele came to say thanks and to introduce himself properly. It turned out that he too was reading law and was going into the final year of his degree at the then Polytechnic of North East London (now the University of East London). He asked me for my telephone number and I asked him if he had a pen. His reply surprised me:

"I don't need one; I will remember it".

Knowing that had his name not been "Dele" as well I would have forgotten it as soon as he uttered it, I was sure that he would forget the number by the time he got home.

To my amazement he called me the following day.

"You wrote it down" I said.

"No, I didn't" he replied.

This was my first exposure to a memory feat of this nature. Not surprisingly Dele walked his exams collecting first class grades across the board. He went on to obtain a first in his degree and won a scholarship to do a masters at Cambridge where he was awarded a first again.

At Bar School he came twenty-first in the order of merit but yet he never made it to the English Bar.

Having, through this process of self analysis and peer group appraisal, discovered my unique strengths and weaknesses, I decided that from the third year on I would play to the former and steer clear of the latter. Technical subjects that demanded understanding were in; subjects that were just full of data and information to be reproduced without real analysis were out.

Using this formula, in my final year my subjects were, Jurisprudence, Tax, Evidence, Constitutional Law and Economics and in the exams I got 2:1s in each subject. When my name appeared as one of the six upper-second class degree awards for that year in law (there were no Firsts awarded), my father felt proud; I only felt relief.

I felt empowered by my degree performance but more so by the understanding that I had acquired of how my mind works. It was much later in life, when all the exams were behind me, that I came to understand the paradox of this memory handicap and my quick grasp of concepts as an aspect of dyslexia.

I, like most people, had always associated dyslexia with those with reading or writing difficulties and I felt that I was certainly not in that category. But as Ronald D Davies explains in his book, *The Gift of Dyslexia*:

"*The most common disabilities of dyslexia occur in reading, writing, spelling or Maths, but there are many others. Each case of dyslexia is different because dyslexia is a self-created condition. No two dyslexics have created it in exactly the same way...Dyslexia is the result of perceptive talent. In some situations the talent becomes a liability. The individual doesn't realise this is happening because use of the talent has become integrated into the thought process".*

If I had known then that Albert Einstein and Richard Branson were also dyslexics, I would have borne the cross of my memory defect with greater assurance. Nevertheless, equipped, as I was, with my new level of self awareness and my upper-second class honours, I was ready for the English Bar. ▓

3. DINNER AT THE INN

I had by the end of the first year of the law degree decided that my strength was in arguing issues and my dyslexia-assisted brain was a great aid in the subtleties of legal problem analysis.

That these were the skills required at the Bar I had deduced from the many law reports that I had read. At the same time I had little knowledge of what solicitors did since they were only ever mentioned as a footnote in the law reports. It was at the beginning of the second year of the law degree that we had to give thought to whether we were going to become barristers or solicitors. I wasted no time in deciding that whatever it was that solicitors did, it was not for me. I needed to be on centre stage standing in the lights. I could see my name in the All England Law Reports of the future: Akindele Ogunetimoju QC.

Finding my voice
There was, however, a major problem. I suffered from acute stage fright. I had come to realise this at secondary school after I had been made Head Boy of Bedford House at Highbury Grove. The school's tradition was for selected sixth formers to deliver a speech to the 1,500-strong school assembly. Mine was a disaster.

The speech itself was a well-written and reasoned discussion of the likely impact of computers on future work patterns. The problem was that only I could hear it even though I had a microphone to speak into. My athletic legs had become weak the moment I rose to address the expectant audience of scholars and staff. It was as if some force had tied my neck in a knot to stop the words coming out and my voice began to quiver.

When, at last, the humiliation was over, I received the ritual applause. I was very conscious of having let my house master, Mr Saunders, down. Hitherto black 6th formers had only made Sports Captain and he had entrusted me with the highest honour of Head Boy only for me to call his judgment into question by this poor display.

The performance haunted me all through the degree programme. How was I going to argue cases in court for a living if I could not speak in public. There were many mock trials and competitions ("moots") both within our law department and against other Universities. I went and watched each in silent admiration of the mock advocates wishing I could be like them while deconstructing their arguments in my head. Thus at this stage of my journey to the English Bar, the world's best advocate was effectively a mute.

It was in the final year of the degree, as Bar School loomed on the near horizon, that I decided to do something about my condition. I went to see my G.P. and made a full and frank confession:

"Doctor, in my mind I am a great public speaker; I know what to say and how to say it but I can't stand up in public and say it".

A problem aired is a problem solved, I have heard say. And so it was. The doctor told me that a lot of professional actors also suffer from stage fright. He prescribed some pretty pink tablets with the instruction that they should be taken one hour before the appointed occasion whenever I had to speak in public.

I hadn't had a real opportunity to test the tablets until an occasion sprung up quite unexpectedly. A moot had been organised by some final-year colleagues for the benefit of some prospective new students. The lecturer who was supposed to preside over the event was indisposed and a new judge had to be identified in time for the moot to start at 2p.m. My strong legal reasoning was acknowledged and respected by my colleagues and, for this reason, I was asked if I would stand in as the judge. Flattery blocked my reasoning and before I knew what I was doing I had agreed. It was only then I remembered my speech impediment and my mind went back to my performance at the Highbury Grove School assembly.

Fortunately my house was only twenty minutes walk from the law precinct. As soon as we were let out of the last lecture at 1p.m., I bombed out of the building and sprinted homewards. Breathless,

I scrambled around my room for the tablets. It was a relief when I saw them in their container. I popped one of the pink beauties and prayed that it would work. I ran back to the law precinct and announced my readiness. Initially I worried that I had not allowed myself the one hour time lag that had been recommended for the magic to work. However, because I was the mock judge and not one of the mock advocates, the timing worked out okay.

When my moment came to deliver my judgment, I felt an excitement but no nerves. I delivered my judgment in a voice and pitch that captivated the audience. I could hear myself and I loved it. The advocate had found his voice and another piece of the jigsaw of my future was in place.

Always wary of chemical drugs, I came across an herb-based alternative called Naturacalm that I used on a number of occasions thereafter but then I realised that my public speaking engagements would not always allow me enough time to pop the magic tablets and so I knew I had to wean myself off them. The knowledge that I could speak in a way that held the attention of an audience coupled with the confidence derived from my strong reasoning and quick thinking enabled me to toss aside the crutches and to walk confidently on to any stage to speak.

The first occasion was later in that final year when I was leading the opposition to a student occupation of the building organised by the National Union of Students. The radical students had barricaded themselves inside the University buildings to stop lectures and tutorials taking place. Although the sit-in had been organised in protest against the admission into the University of one Nick Harrington, said to be the leader of the National Front (an organisation whose political objective was to repatriate black people like myself out of Britain), I did not see it as a sensible response when exams were approaching. It looked like a good laugh for the sons of the soil who could afford to be indifferent to their studies; it was not for the likes of me for whom everything depended on our academic attainments.

I made an impassioned speech for the discontinuance of the occupation pleading the special case of the overseas students, who the Thatcher Government had by now decreed should be charged at commercial rates for their tuition. The idea of home students (whose fees were being paid by taxpayers, many of whom and whose children would never have the opportunity to read for a degree) preventing others from exercising their right to attend classes, grated with me. When my drug-free speech left the self-indulgent majority unmoved, I led the opposition in crossing the picket lines. It was on another occasion, later in life, that I got the opportunity to deal, in my own way, with those who harboured sentiments like Mr Harrington.

The members of the Campaign for United Kingdom Conservatism were not racists like the National Front or the BNP; they were just nationalists. The difference was that they loved their nation and they did so without resenting others. They had no problem with sharing their nation with others who had come to live with them like the immigrants from the Commonwealth. Their angst was with those behind the "Euro-plot": the conspiracy, as they saw it, between the Roman Catholic Church and multinational corporations to merge the free-standing nations of Europe into a political union to be known as the United States of Europe with its capital in Brussels and its spiritual home set in the Vatican City, Rome.

At the invitation of Sir Richard Body MP, a philosopher and barrister who I had come to know, I had written an article for the *Salisbury Review* titled "Nigeria and Europe: Not So Distant Cousins" in which I had highlighted the democratic deficit that results when democracy is sought to be practiced on too large a scale. The article had become sweet nectar for the Eurosceptics and on reading it the chairman of the Campaign for United Kingdom Conservatisim had asked if I would agree to speak at one of their bi-annual conferences at Oxford University.

We had agreed that I should attend their upcoming conference as an observer to get a better feel for who they were and how they operated before my own speech at the next session. Perhaps because I was still taking in the magnificence of the University of Oxford I got to the lecture hall a little late. Though I tried to make my entry with the minimum of disturbance to the speaker who was in full flow, disturbance there was since I was the lone black in the sea of white faces. Once I had taken my seat the chairman nodded at me in silent acknowledgement and welcome.

The speaker, a law professor at the university, was delivering a paper titled "Christianity and the English Common Law". Jurisprudence having been my favorite subject on the law degree, I was very interested in what he had to say. He was explaining how the moral values of any community are reflected in their basic laws and how the core principles of the English Common law are to be found in Christian ideals. He supported his thesis as he went along with quotations from the bible. Then he let rip:

"But now we have heathens in our Parliament making our laws. What is to become of the English Common Law when we have Muslim members of the Parliament of this country?".

As he soaked in the applause I resolved to take him on for by this time I had taught myself the parts of British history that had been left off the syllabus at O and A Level. When the chairman called for questions, I was the first to raise my hand. I began by commending the insight he had given into the connection between faith and law and then asked him what his views were on the British Empire.

"You mean what we did?" he asked.

"No", I replied. I decided to short-circuit the cross-examination. "I mean when you speak of heathens in your Parliament, you seem to have overlooked the fact that these heathens were happy in their own country until your grandfathers and great-grandfathers took it upon themselves to go and visit them".

I went on: "I need to share something with you which is that in cultures like mine, if you decide to come and visit me, it would be regarded as rude if I didn't return the visit and that is what we immigrants are doing".

By this point the audience, who had applauded him with such enthusiasm,were now laughing with me. I finished him off by saying: "But it is in the bible that you have been quoting from: 'Love thy neighbour as thyself and do unto others as you will have them do unto you'",

His attempted rejoinder: "But that doesn't mean............ " was lost in the applause. The chairman ended the encounter by saying: "Well now you have met Mr Ogunetimoju who is our speaker for our next meeting".

The English Bar

A career at the English Bar is the ultimate indulgence for a lawyer. The chambers (offices) from which the barristers operate, set within the lush grounds of the four medieval Inns of Court (Middle Temple, Inner Temple, Gray's Inn and Lincoln's Inn) are a leisurely stroll from the superior courts, the High Court and the Court of Appeal, in which they perform their skills as advocates. The judges before whom they argue their cases, being almost exclusively drawn from the circle of former barristers, relate to them as members of a sacred order. The better chambers boast a commensurate library, but all chambers can draw on the resources of the Inn library, where the laws, not just of England but virtually the whole of the old British Empire can be found.

The grounds and the library aside, the barrister's work environment is spartan in its efficiency. They carry neither clients nor files and very few staff. Their service being provided to the solicitors' firms by whom they are instructed, the barristers' sets have no need for the costs and expense of modern glass-fronted offices, or for luxuriously furnished waiting and conference rooms for clients. Since the key to obtaining instructions is to be known to solicitors rather than lay clients, marketing strategy goes little beyond an occasional invitation to the partners in the solicitors' firms to join them for the odd glass of choice wines. No need for expensive brochures and marketing executives. What is left by way of overheads is shared between the members of chambers by way of a chambers' rent

When it comes to the work itself, with experienced lawyers from the instructing solicitors having narrowed down the issues and organized the paperwork, the barrister can surf from one case to another with the barest minimum of staffing. If on reviewing the brief from the instructing solicitors more information or evidence is needed, it is simply a matter of asking the solicitor to get it.

When it comes to the matter of charges, it is left to the clerk to negotiate these with instructing solicitors. Having an intermediary to discuss the earthly matter of money has the advantage that the clerk can pitch for A Level of fees that the barristers themselves would have difficulty in arguing for. The clerks being typically of the same stock as estate agents and, as such, having no independent grasp of the substance of the work involved, simply aim to get as much above the "not-less-than" amount that the barrister has given them. A rule of convenience says that barristers cannot sue for their fees and so it is the responsibility of the instructing solicitors to collect the barrister's fees for him and to act as his debt collector if appropriate. In fact the credit risk of the client is passed to the solicitor as it is the solicitor that the barrister holds responsible for his fees with the possibility of the solicitor being black-listed if the fees are not settled.

Once the barrister has finished his work on a case he sends

the files back to the instructing solicitor to dispose of them for him. If the case is lost it is the solicitor that deals with the client's disappointment. With a spirit of brotherhood rather than partnership governing relationships within chambers, and with the work being a purely intellectual exercise free from the burdens of sentiment that might come from direct interaction with the client, it is possible for members of chambers to appear against each other on opposite sides of the same case.

The cream on the strawberries of a barrister's life is the knowledge that the Bar is the gateway through which those who will be the judges in England and Wales must, typically, pass. Each good set of chambers will be able to boast past members who are past or serving judges. It is this close and very special relationship with the judiciary that members of the Bar enjoy that underlies the Bar's claim to seniority in relation to their solicitor colleagues. The outward sign of that claim was the historic monopoly on the right to wear wigs in court with the judges. This is the culture of the English Bar as it is and as it has been for hundreds of years.

Little wonder then that if by the time you started Bar School you were not eating, drinking and speaking like a judge to be, because you had not been to the right schools, you very quickly found yourself being caught up in the culture. When this exercise in cultural assimilation is taken on too enthusiastically by ethnic minority lawyers it can produce pure theatre.

Back then, as if to keep out the uninvited, the Bar School (otherwise known as the Inns of Court School of Law) was tucked away in a narrow passage off High Holborn. Quite simply, if you weren't told where it was you would never know. Even when you were standing in the passage, the only thing that betrayed its presence was the crest of the school, which incorporated within its design the crest of the four Inns of Court whose lawyers it was responsible for educating.

Each Inn has its own reputation amongst the student population. Inner Temple was stuffy, Middle Temple was stuffier and Gray's Inn was the stuffiest. I was told that at Gray's Inn dinners, students would be challenged to propose a toast to the Queen and to apply for permission to smoke. Being neither a royalist nor a smoker, there was no way I was going there. If I had to eat twenty-four dinners, one of the then pre-conditions to being called to the Bar, I needed a more relaxed environment within which to suffer this compulsory feeding on English roast and brussel sprouts washed down with glasses of port.

Lincoln's Inn, I had been told, was less traditional and this sounded like the best option for me. Dinner at the Inn was an experience far removed from lunch at Highbury Grove where, in order to maximize the time we had for football during the lunch hour, we gobbled our puddings first and stuffed the chips into our fish-finger or sausage rolls before stuffing the combination into our blazer pockets for consumption after the game. The array of stainless steel cutlery and wine glasses was bewildering. Knowing which to use, and for what, distinguished those who belonged from those who were merely aspiring. It was perhaps their sense of belonging that enabled the public school boys to do something that the rest of us would never have dared such as to let off a loud fart as the Benchers (the senior members of the Inn of Court) were taking it in turns to bow out to bring the grand dinner occasion to a close.

The choice of Lincoln's Inn was also influenced by the fact that great names like Gandhi and Lord Denning were of Lincoln's as was the then Prime Minister, Margaret Thatcher, oil paintings of whom adorned the grand hall. I also thought that because Lincoln's was the centre of the Chancery Bar where I planned to practice, my membership of the Inn would help to secure my passage into Chancery practice.

Bar School was an uplifting experience. I felt that I had made it into a finishing school for gladiators – those who would one day engage in intellectual combat in the Coliseum that was the House of Lords before the Law Lords. Throughout that year, until the results came out, I carried myself like the anointed one amongst them. I was no respecter of the reputation of academic institutions. Armed with the knowledge of my strengths and weaknesses, I sought out the most technically challenging options on offer. They were reputed to be Landlord and Tenant Law and Legal Aspects of International Trade. In the end, because of my resolve to be a chancery barrister, I took the be Landlord and Tenant option only and went instead for Practical Conveyancing as the second option.

My fascination with the various aspects of the law on land ownership in England was peculiar coming as I was from a culture where the ownership of land might be claimed by a community but never by an individual. In Aiyede land that "belonged" to members of the Ogunetimoju family belonged to the family but was occupied by the individual with the family's consent. The land was simply there for you to use, not for you to sell, lease, licence or mortgage. The attitude of the community is that it was there before you and it will be there after you.

That this attitude to land ownership was not unique to us but was typical of almost all indigenous peoples – the true conservationists of this world – was confirmed in a discussion that I had with a Native-American judge whom I later met in Seattle. He told the tale that had been passed down to him of how when the white men came the first arrivals were hungry and in need of shelter having been on the oceans for so long. He told of how his forebears fed them and nursed them back to health and how, when the white men were strong enough again they returned to their lands only to come back with more of their own and now claimed to own the land. He explained how this was strange to his people because in their way of life (to use his words): *"A man cannot own the land any more than he can own a piece of the sky"*. His people clearly did not appreciate the jurisprudence of English land law that possession is 9/10ths of ownership.

The conceptual difficulties were confirmed on a later trip when I met a lawyer in Phoenix Arizona who was from the Navaho tribe. She explained how real estate law (land law in America), based as it was on western concepts of land ownership, was the one subject that had almost prevented her from becoming one of the few of her kind who had made it to the Arizona State Bar. "I just couldn't get my head around it", she said. After all, a great Native-American chief, Crazy Horse, had said: *"One does not sell the earth upon which the people walk"*. When, in 2007, it was reported that the Russians had claimed ownership of the Arctic seabed after their submarine crew had successfully planted their country's flag in the seabed 14,000 feet below the North Pole, I could not but wonder who best deserved to wear the "crazy" label.

A few of the other black students had also gone for the more challenging options. One such was Vince Phillips, who was there with me on the Landlord and Tenant Option and who had also elected for Legal Aspects of International Trade (he had obtained an upper-second from South Bank Polytechnic) and who I related to well. His fine looks had earned him the salutation "Too-Smooth-Vince". Samuel Kale, a.k.a. 'Esquire', was a very colourful other. From English-speaking Cameroon (the former German colony having been split as part of the spoils of the First World War between Britain and France), he dressed the part of the English barrister better than the sons-of-the-soil themselves: the braces, the brogues and the handkerchief in the top pocket were sine qua non. Another was a mixed race fellow by the name of Robert Hunter who had obtained a first from Leeds University and who had taken the same two options as myself. His manner of speaking was just a touch too polished for me at that stage and so I couldn't relate to him.

While the options gave me the chance to avoid my weak flank, the compulsory subjects did not. I knew from the start that Civil Procedure and Criminal Procedure, two memory-intensive courses that most other students looked to for their salvation, were going to be my headache when the exams came round. Meantime I had other headaches to deal with, the biggest of which was finding a pupilage.

The hardest part of qualifying to practice at the Bar is finding somewhere to practice from. I really did buy the script that the Bar was the ultimate in meritocracy – a citadel into which only the most capable advocates would be admitted and where only the best would wear the laurels. But dreams are so easily bought into by those who lack any experience.

The restrictive practices that prevail in the profession mean that however much you rated your potential, you could never get to practice at the Bar unless someone on the inside was prepared to let you in. Yes, you could be called to the Bar by passing your exams and eating your prescribed dinners as many were, but only the few would be chosen for the opportunity to practice. The first stage in being chosen was to complete a twelve-month period of pupilage.

The number of vacancies for pupilage was always greatly outstripped by the number of would-be pupils and so the frenzied scramble for pupilage began almost as soon as the Bar School year began. For those who were truly connected, through a father, grandfather or godfather, pupilage was in the bag long before the others arrived at the starting line. Thus you had the anomalous situation where a critical but scarce opportunity to practice at the Bar was shared out before the candidates had been tested on their aptitude for the profession. There were instances where students who had secured pupilage then did not make it through the Bar Exams while many more who did pass the exams could not find pupilage.

I was in the latter group and I wasn't amused by the experience.

It was a betrayal of the spirit of competition of which education is supposed to be the most robust. I had made countless applications without so much as a sniff at an interview for pupilage. In one case I had posted my CV and covering letter on one day and received my curt letter of rejection two days later. Looking back now, it is clear that my quest was always a hopeless one. I was applying for admission to the Chancery Bar, having dismissed the Criminal and Common Law Bar as not being sufficiently intellectually robust, yet my schooling was wrong, my alma mater was wrong, my race was wrong and my name was wrong.

I have come to learn that in life, sometimes the best decisions are made for you by circumstances and events rather than by you. So it was with regards to my exclusion from the Bar. Hard as it can be to get into the legal profession in England, getting in is but a stroll in the park compared with staying in. It is because, like much else in life, everything revolves around human relationships. This is the fundamental difference between being a good law student and being a good legal practitioner.

An exam is an un-emotional contest between yourself, the clock and your syllabus; these are all factors within your own mastery. The world of work on the other hand is all about the inter-personal: barristers get their work from solicitors that they know or from solicitors that people that they know know. Solicitors get their work from clients that they know and clients give their work to solicitors that they know and so the cycle continues. Thus the key to a successful practice is a pre-existing network or the ability to build a network very quickly on which a reputation can then be built. This is the critical career guidance that most law students never receive before starting out.

Had I somehow managed to secure a Chancery pupilage, and assuming then that I had somehow demonstrated a good enough business case to secure a position within the law chambers (a tenancy) ahead of the other pupils competing for this holy grail, I have no doubt that I would have been mired in so much debt that I would have thrown in the towel very quickly. This was because I had no network that I could look to as a supply-line for work in the early critical stages. In such a situation you are dependent on the goodwill of the clerks to the chambers. It is they who, when a stray instruction comes in, will recommend one junior barrister or the other, and the recommendation will depend on the clerk's own personal relationship with the barrister candidates. As most social relationships in England go, it would normally turn on how you get on after work over a drink or two.

In any case the financial challenges of the Bar School year were hard enough for me let alone the thought of moving from there straight into self-employed status as a barrister. I had seen the writing on the wall in my early applications for pupilage and I had started thinking about alternatives. The one that then appealed to me was going home to try my luck at the Nigerian Bar. I was encouraged by the fact that Oba Nsugbe and Tunde Folawiyo, both of whom I met at Bar school, were also going to do the Nigerian Bar.

It was to be another challenge for me. I had not lived in Nigeria since I had been brought out at age of seven and three quarters and I had only been back twice on holiday in more recent years. Tunde Folawiyo was reputed to be from one of the richest families in Nigeria, Oba Nsugbe had reasonable family support, but apart from accommodation, I knew I would be very much dependent on my own resources. One good habit that I had developed was that having identified a problem I would always go on to find a solution.

It was in Christmas break of the Bar School year that I started a night security shift in order to begin the process of saving the money that I would live on in Nigeria. It meant giving up my social life but I was hardy enough to do it. It also meant turning up to tutorials on Monday morning after a twelve-hour night shift and nodding off in the middle of the class to the amusement of others, but there was no alternative. There was many a day during that Bar School year that I had to content myself with watching others eat in the canteen because I couldn't afford the experience myself.

The Bar course itself was intense only in terms of the volume of work rather than its complexity. Although there was a greater practical content, particularly around court procedures and the drafting of pleadings and opinions, much of it was still very much like the degree course. The practical exercises in the form of mock cross-examinations and pleas took place in the evenings in the court rooms at the High Court under the instruction of a practicing barrister. This was the part of the syllabus that I enjoyed most although the irony of my having failed my spoken English O Level was not lost on me. Alas there was no opportunity to remove this blot on my scholarly record as the practical exercises had no bearing on your marks in the Bar Finals.

The Finals came round astonishingly quickly. I prepared in the same way as I had devised for the final year degree exams. I started early on the procedure subjects and all others that tested memory and left the more technically-challenging subjects to last. Once again the expectations that others had of me were high since I had become the favourite port of call for those who were experiencing difficulty with some of the concepts and problems. The procedure subjects had diluted my overall score. Once more Shaun Wallace was there. Though he had finished the year before, such was his passion for black educational achievement that he was there on the day the results came out to see how I and others had done. True to form he started at the top with the names of those who had attained firsts only to find my name lower down nestled amongst the third-class honours.

My emotions were mixed on the day that the results were released. My last hopes of securing a pupilage rested on a strong performance in the Bar Exam. This hope had now gone. Even so I was relieved that I had made it through both the criminal and civil procedure papers. These were the papers in which failure was a real possibility. My friend from London Metropolitan, Justin Baron, a tremendous legal mind who I believe suffered from the same dyslexia-related handicap, did not make it through on account of the same procedure subjects. When he couldn't get through those papers at the second time of asking, what would have been a successful career at the Bar got only as far as the position of Chief Clerk to Magistrates in Wales.

The achievement was a great one in my father's eyes. This was the Golden Fleece that he had left his country in quest of but which he had not secured. By not sparing the liberal lashes of the whip he had got the wayward boy over the finish line. For some reason that I cannot now recall, he wasn't there on the day my name was called to the Bar but Mum was, just as she had been when I arrived from Nigeria at Heathrow Airport.

The Bar Council Handbook contains a stark, and slightly smug, warning to those reading to become barristers: *"Many are called but few are chosen"*.

I had been called to the English Bar but not been chosen and so it was back to Heathrow to head home for the Nigerian Bar. ▓

4. BACK
TO LAGOS

I arrived in Lagos on the weekend of 30 September 1985 ahead of the Monday date for enrolment at the Bar School.

The party that Nigeria had called on the back of the strong oil revenues of the late 1970s and early 1980s was still going on. The bubble had burst but the impact had yet to be felt. The exchange rate was still officially N1 to £1 although the black market rate of N7 to £1 was already signaling the direction in which things were heading.

Nigerians were still feeling like kings of the world and they were still being made to feel that way by the traders from across the world anxious to relieve them of the burden of their suddenly found wealth. After all one of the ministers had declared; "Nigeria's problem is not money but how to spend it". Meantime the stench of the open gutter was still there in Omididun Street and Aiyede still had no tarred roads, pipe-borne water or electricity.

I was staying with Ms Titi Shonubi, a friend of my mother, who always stayed with us in London whenever she visited. She had a well-furnished two-bedroom upper-floor apartment in Alhaji Masha area of Surulere on the Lagos Mainland. Surulere at this time qualified as a middle-class area and Alhaji Masha was within the nicer part of the district. The open guttering in the area was less intrusive on the senses than in other areas of Lagos.

Knowing how things worked in Lagos, Ms Shonubi advised me to take a trip down to the Law School ahead of the enrolment on Monday. It was sound advice. Nigeria is hot and wet half the year and hot and dry for the rest; there is no "in between". Late September when I arrived was the end of the rainy season and this was a blazing hot and dry Sunday.

The Law School was located in an island to the south of the Nigerian mainland that the British colonial government had named after its Queen Victoria. The building itself was much more imposing than the Bar School in England. Set within generous grounds overlooking the lagoon that separated Victoria Island and Ikoyi Island, it was a place that Nigerians of all walks of life aspired to go to.

Having noted the route and surveyed the scene, I walked back to the road junction to look for a taxi. It was then that I came face to face with the reality of the extremes of wealth in Nigeria. A Mercedes turned into the road from Ozumba Mbadiwe Road.

"Del Boy"! I heard the nickname I had been given at Bar School in England. It was Tunde Folawiyo.

I explained my Sunday mission and that I was now looking for a taxi to take me back to Surulere. He apologized that he was under some time pressure to get to where he was going. As he was giving his apologies another Mercedes turned into the road from the opposite direction. He flagged down the second car which he had recognized as one of his father's and he instructed the driver to take me home.

"Welcome to Nigeria!", I thought.

The lawyer holds special pride of place in the esteem of Nigerians and we, as a people, seem to have a natural aptitude for the subject much as Asians appear to have a natural gift for maths. Whatever the explanation, every retired brigadier, permanent secretary, bank executive or Miss Nigeria seeks his or her ultimate fulfilment in a law degree followed by attendance at the Nigerian Law School. As it is for those on their second career so it is for those on their first. If you didn't have a gift for maths and the sciences to get into medical school or to read accountancy, law was the natural selection. The competition for places on the law degree and subsequently for the then one Law School was, therefore, intense.

The predilection for reading law is a touch ironic given the perception of general lawlessness with which the country and its leaders are regarded. Although at this time a new military regime, under General Buhari and Major Tunde Idiagbon, had seized the reins of government with the declared intent of restoring order and discipline, it was still very much a free-for-all atmosphere. Nigerians were on a high. It would take a lot more than the War Against Indiscipline that the soldiers had declared in the country (under which Nigerians were made, under the terror of the soldiers' whips, to queue, to obey traffic lights and not to drive on the wrong side of dual carriageways) to sober them up.

The War Against Indiscipline had clearly not been declared to the hearing of the students who showed up to enroll at the Nigerian Law School that Monday morning. Word had been passed down by members of the Alumni that best seats in the house were in the main auditorium where you could see the lecturers with your own eyes. If you didn't get a seat there, you would be left with only the virtual encounter with the lecturers through speakers and erratic TV monitors in the ante-rooms.

The scrum to get through the single door entrance into the main hall that I witnessed that first Monday morning has not yet been seen at Twickenham Rugby football ground. It was sheer bedlam the sight of which was made worse by the fact that all male students were required to wear suits and the ladies were similarly formally attired. The scrum that day involved as many women as men. Heads were to be found between legs and bums over feet. I laughed until I cried. It was a hilariously bad advert for my 'learned friends-to-be'. Sanity was restored the second day when the battles over the seating arrangements had been won and lost.

Unlike Bar School in England where you wore whatever pleased you, typically jeans and a tee-shirt, at the Nigerian Law School you dressed to impress. Each morning you groomed yourself to look like the lawyer that you were aspiring to be. Your neighbours had to know that you were at Law School; the taxi driver and anyone else that you might encounter on your journey had to be in no doubt that you were a "Learned Friend-in-the-making". When it comes to looking good, it is hard to think of any people that can do it better than Nigerians whatever their budget. If the men looked sharp, the ladies were mind-blowing, particularly for those of us who had lived too long in Britain where women are always a little too restrained in expressing themselves in colour.

All the signs were that this was not going to be a place for serious study but then again I wasn't complaining about the substitute of serious fun. By day and by night there were beach parties, house parties and club parties.

I had been introduced to high living by the Nigerian girlfriend that I had in London just before I flew down. Although a student, from what appeared to be a poor family, she was getting enough money from her "rich uncle" to live in Abbey Road, Swiss Cottage and to sleep on satin sheets. No sooner had I landed than I resolved that I needed another and no sooner had we enrolled than I found her.

She waltzed by me in her "bones" with a perfect set of gleaming white teeth set against her dark brown skin. I took even more notice when later the same day she cruised past me in her new Mercedes E Class. That was it, I decided I needed to have me some fun. Her father, a big time businessman, had given her the Mercedes as her graduation present. She was a nice girl but I never met her father and fortunately her father never met me. I say fortunately because her father had a reputation as an old "player" and one thing about old players is that they don't like anyone playing with their pretty young things and certainly not in their house. I understood that he didn't take prisoners.

Still we played. He always flew to his home town on Friday evening to return on Monday morning. As soon as his driver drove him out of the compound headed for the airport she would call me to come on down and the house became ours until Monday morning when we would head off to Law School together. So the game went until one day the man's cook, who was forever high on Ogogoro (high strength local gin), grassed us up. The wicked old man set the trap. He headed off one Friday evening in his usual way but instead of flying out of town he simply hung out and then headed back home. Fortunately for me the relationship had been brought to an end the week before and that's why I am here to tell the tale.

Those of us who graduated abroad were put together in the same group, Group A5. In a country where everything foreign is presumed to be better than the local equivalents, there was no shortage of airs and graces, and we certainly appeared to be the ones that the ladies wanted to know. It was no doubt because of this, to take us down a peg or two, that the phenomenon known as Fidelis Oditah was unleashed on us.

We didn't take him at all seriously at first. Neither his stature nor his dress style commanded our attention as he waddled into our lecture room. He had been assigned to lecture us on the Nigerian Legal System. Word quickly went round that he had only finished the Bar School himself in the previous intake but that the first class honours that he attained had been unprecedented and he had performed a similar feat at the University of Lagos.

We the A5 boys were of a mind that we were not so easily impressed. That was until he was about ten minutes into his monologue. Then it struck us that although he was reading from the textbook, there were no books or papers anywhere near him. Awe slowly displaced cynicism and then began the speculation as to whether he was using some form of wireless tape recording system. He wasn't. Oditah continued like this for the whole hour without missing a word or a full stop. When the hour was up, he simply got up and left. The whole of the class was now in an uproar over the feat they had just witnessed. Oditah would go on to receive a Commonwealth scholarship to do a masters at Oxford University before practising at the English Bar.

Daughter of Biafra
It was immediately after my narrow escape that I met my wife-to-be, Esther Ebelechukwu Ene. She had graduated at the University of Nigeria, Nsukka, Igbo land. The Law School had brought her to Lagos, Yoruba land. The Igbos and the Yoruba had been on opposite sides of the "Nigerian civil war". Except that to call it a civil war is to oversimplify what the war was about.

Prior to 1900 there was no place called "Nigeria" and no people known as "Nigerians". The people who are known as Nigerians knew themselves as Yoruba, Hausa, Igbo, Ijaw, Kanuri, Tiv, Edo, Fulani etc. Their lands were as distinct from each other as their languages.

It was in 1900, following the 1884 Berlin Conference at which the African continent was parceled out between the great powers of Europe, that the British Colonial office decided to make Nigeria by merging these hitherto ethnically and politically disparate peoples for ease of colonial administration. At first they decided to make two Nigerias: a Northern Nigeria made up predominately of Islamic territories and a Southern Nigerian made up in the most part of Christian territories. However, in the face of the exigencies of the First World War, the British Government decided, in 1914, to merge the largely Islamic Northern Nigeria with the predominantly Christian Southern Nigeria by colonial fiat.

The parties to this arranged and enforced marriage had still not found love for each other by the end of the Second World War when the British and French Governments were compelled, by the U.S. Government, to release their colonies as a pre-condition for receiving Marshall Plan aid to help rebuild their own war-ravaged countries.

It is in the nature of marriages that are not based on the voluntary union of the parties but on the influence and calculations of third parties that when that external glue is removed, the marriage falls apart unless it can again be held together by a new force; until that new force is firmly in control a power struggle will inevitably ensue between those who have been so brought together in union. So it was that in the run up to Nigeria's independence in 1960 the jostling began as to which of the big three originally distinct and rival nations (the Yoruba, the Hausa-Fulani and the Igbo) was to take over as top dog from the departing colonial masters.

Although the British colonial government put the country through the motions of independence elections, it did not leave the outcome to chance or to the Nigerian people. This is how Obafemi Awolowo, one of the main contestants in that election, explained it in his book *The People's Republic*:

The climax to all these manoeuvres came when a Northern leader was invited to form a new administration for the Federation, on the basis of the election results. There were altogether 312 seats in the House of Representatives. Three main parties had contested the election. The following of one of the parties was confined to the North, whilst the other two enjoyed country-wide support. The results of the election began to trickle in after midnight on 12 December 1959. On 14 December 1959, when the other two parties discovered that neither of them was going to have an overall majority in the Federal Parliament, they immediately commenced negotiation for a coalition between them. This became known to the public; and on 15 December 1959, whilst the coalition negotiation was still in progress, and when the score of the Northern party was only 116 as against 150 for the other two parties, a Northern leader was invited to form a new administration.

Because of transport difficulties in the North, the final results were not known until 19 December 1959, when the scores were, for the Northern party 142 seats, for the other two parties 162, and for independents 8. By 17 December 1959, however, one of the other two parties had concluded a coalition agreement with the Northern party which, by the grace of the British, was already irrevocably installed on the throne of power on 15 December 1959.

The swift action of the British in calling upon the Northern party to form a new administration, thereby forestalling a coalition agreement between the other political parties, each of which was led by a Southern politician of the 'agitator' type, was explicable only on the ground that they (the British) were determined to hand over power in 1960 to a Northern political leader.

So the cunning old British Lion had, behind the scenes, engineered another marriage of convenience between the Hausa-Fulani and the Igbos giving the Hausa-Fulani the role of senior partner with the Igbos as junior partners and leaving the Yoruba in opposition. The power equation having been thus reduced to two dimensions, it was not long before the two top dogs clashed over the issue as to who was to be on top. The fact that the first successful oil well had been drilled in 1956 and a big oil field had been discovered in 1965 in the Niger Delta (eastern Nigeria) where the Igbos held sway, was not a small influence on the political alignments both internally and externally.

On 15 January, 1966, an Igbo-led military coup overturned the pecking order that the British Government had ordained by taking out, somewhat selectively, the top Hausa-Fulani leaders and putting Igbos on top with an Igbo man, Major-General Johnson Aguiyi-Ironsi, as military ruler. In the belief that they were now the top dogs, the new Igbo-led Federal Government now proceeded to dismantle the three-region federal structure and to make the centre all powerful.

The move backfired when, within six months on 29 July, 1966, the Hausa-Fulani (again it is said, with the help of the former colonial masters) organised a counter-coup, led by then Lieutenant-Colonel Murtala Mohammed, to restore the original pecking order. Aguiyi-Ironsi had lasted just 194 days in power. The Hausa-Fulani political leadership, now wary of their former junior partners, not only sought to cozy up with the Yoruba but also initiated a vengeful series of pogroms against Igbos living in the North.

It was these pogroms, and the refusal of the Hausa-Fulani-controlled Federal Government to honour the terms of a power-sharing peace accord that had been brokered in Aburi, Ghana (the effect of which would have been to restore the old tripod-federation with a weaker centre), that pushed Esther's people to declare their wish to free themselves from the forced union called Nigeria to form, with the other nations in eastern Nigeria, the independent country of Biafra. Thus began the Biafran war on 6 July, 1967.

Esther had only just celebrated her first birthday when the vicious war broke out. The starvation of her people had been an instrument of that war and it was said that a Yoruba man was the Minister of Finance that had initiated the policy. As my Nigeria political education grew, I came to realize that the charge that had been leveled against him was highly questionable and looked more like part of the propaganda to enable the Hausa-Fulani-controlled Federal Government to play off the Igbos against the Yoruba to prevent a united front emerging in southern Nigeria.

My skepticism was reinforced when, on further enquiry, I discovered that, in a war that was clearly a fight between the Hausa-Fulani and the Igbos for hegemony, it was a Yoruba General, Olusegun Obasanjo, that was wheeled out to accept the surrender of the Biafran army on 13 January, 1970.

The man at whom the muck had been thrown was the lawyer, philosopher and writer, Chief Obafemi Awolowo, earlier mentioned. He had been charged and imprisoned for high treason by the Hausa-Fulani/Igbo-led administration before the troubles started. When the Igbo-led administration which took over missed the opportunity to release him from prison so as to win him and his followers to their side in the struggle against their former alliance partners, the latter did not miss the trick when they recovered the reins of power in the counter-coup.

However, it was obvious to me that the strategists on the side of the Nigerian government had post-war internal relations in mind when they parked the poor fellow in the Ministry of Finance as part of the terms of his release from prison. There he was a sitting scapegoat for the starvation offensive that the government was to launch against the Igbos. The strategy worked so well that General Murtala Mohammed, who is believed to have committed acts bordering on war crimes, against the Igbos, would re-emerge through another coup on 29 July, 1975, as the military ruler of Nigeria and national hero. (His rule was to last 199 days, just five days longer than that of Johnson Aguiyi-Ironsi, whom he had overthrown on 29 July, 1966. There is something about Murtala Mohammed and the 29th of July that I haven't yet worked out!)

Meantime Awolowo emerged from the stage as the villain. Through reading his autobiography *Awo*, his many speeches and his schorlarly work *The People's Republic*, I would come to know that his was a political mind that was on par with Prime Ministers Lee Kuan Yew of Singapore and Dr. Mahathir Mohamad of Malaysia. From his performance as Premier of the old Western Region of Nigeria, most fair commentators acknowledge that the story of Nigeria would have been very different had his talents not fallen prey to the wider geo-political calculations of the Cold War.

Though the Igbos fought valiantly, making their own bombs and guns (an hitherto unheard-of feat in black Africa), and though millions were lost in the bloody war, Biafra never came to be. The Igbo warriors did not at the time realize that they were fighting for an impossible prize: viz. to break out of the colonial boundaries that had been fixed by the European Powers in 1884 from which none of the "tribes" of Africa has yet escaped. This is how Esther came to be at the Nigerian Law School. All the same this daughter of a Biafran had never planned on marrying a Yoruba man, even one who had been a prize winner in History at Highbury Grove Secondary School, London, England!

Our eyes had met on a couple of occasions as her group took over our tutorial room, but the Christmas break intervened before I could make my move. When we resumed in January I was on the lookout. Early in that new term, our paths crossed again and, as she was leaving the library, I was "in there", as they say.

"Hi, what's your name"? I asked.

"What's yours first"? was the confident and dignified reply.

From then on we were an item. During the week she stayed at YWCA Hall at Moloney, Lagos Island and we spoke each evening by phone; at the weekend she would stay in Surulere. Her mother declared that her first child could not marry a Yoruba man and, for her part, my mother was firm in her conviction that she could not have an Igbo woman as her only daughter-in-law. Both women would later come to share their husbands' outlook that what mattered was our own judgment.

False Economy

I was having more fun than I had ever known since leaving Nigeria as a child. So much fun that I didn't realise how quickly the year had passed. Before I knew it the exams were upon us.

The Nigeria Law School exams were even more a test of memory than the Bar exams in England because the law books being, almost exclusively, books written by English academics, in England, with reference to the laws of England, were beyond the reach of most home students. The Law School library was scarcely better endowed than the body of students.

The lecturers sought to compensate for this handicap by producing, and handing out, copious lecture notes, but given that one of the core skills of a lawyer is the ability to conduct research, this was a bankrupt substitute. It became common knowledge that all that was expected of you was to commit the copious handouts to memory and to reproduce them in the exam as faithfully as time permitted.

There being no scope for independent research, there was no reward for original thinking. In fact, far from being rewarded, you would be marked down for having the audacity to diverge from the learned lecturer's viewpoint. Blasphemy! Those who excelled in the exams were those who had formidable memories like Tunde, from London, and my own Esther.

The exams were followed by a six week period of attachment with a law firm. This was the equivalent of pupilage at the English Bar.

Unlike the arrangements in England, there was reasonable assurance that every student would find a place to get the experience he/she needed. Through Ms Shonubi, I got a position for three weeks with Messrs Giwa & Co, a sole practice in Breadfruit Street, in downtown Lagos. I spent most of the three weeks pestering poor old Chief Giwa for work I could do for him of which he had not a lot. With time on my hands I decided to use some if it to take a closer look at the realities of the Nigerian economy.

For this, I didn't have far to go. The chambers sat on top of a small street market. The stifling heat in the small, cramped office meant that the windows had to remain open. Through these vents I got a fair idea as to who was selling what, and from where, complete with the aroma of whatever it was they were selling. A few twists and turns from the Chambers would take you into the mega-, and maze-like, Balogun market where all the produce of the West, Arabia, and the Orient could be found.

These regular and extended lunch-time strolls through the market convinced me that in spite of my country's claim to be "the giant of Africa", there wasn't all that much going on in the

Nigerian economy: everything on offer was made everywhere but in Nigeria.

The Nigerian economy was (and still is) the ultimate consumer economy in which my people take pride in consuming what people of other countries take pride in producing. It is a spendthrift lifestyle that we fund through the largesse of oil money – a finite resource. We are busy treating receipts from capital as renewable income. Hardly do we spare a thought to what we will live on when the oil runs out. I could now see why Lagos had always been top of the list in the London billboards offering tax-free exports.

My A Level economics was enough to tell me that the standard of living that middle-class Nigerians were then enjoying could not be sustained. The officially declared parity in the exchange rate between the Naira and sterling was already being mocked by a black market rate of N7 to £1. I had no doubt that the mockery had much further to go. What concerned me more was the inability of my people, not least a group of economics undergraduates with whom I debated the issue at this time, to see the signs.

I had come to Ibadan, 125KM north of Lagos, the former political capital of Yoruba land, to do the second half of my post-Law School attachment. My uncle, Dr Ijose (he who had taken me back to Aiyede on my first "holiday" to Nigeria) had arranged for me to spend three weeks in one of the leading chambers in the rusty city. It was a chance for me to know a little more of Yoruba land proper which is different from cosmopolitan Lagos.

Ibadan is a city of the most extreme contrasts. There was Ibadan proper, the dusty and rusty urban sprawl; and then there was the Institute of Tropical Agriculture, a research institute carved out of Ibadan by the Americans and where what Ibadan, and indeed Nigeria, could look like is showcased with glistening lakes and lush green lawns complete with pink flamingoes and white swans.

The University of Ibadan was one of the other premier Universities in Nigeria being, along with the University of Lagos and Esther's University of Nigeria Nsukka, one of the first three in the country. On a weekend visit with a cousin, my "English accent" had provoked a debate on the world at large and the Nigerian economy in particular. My viewpoint that the Nigerian economy lacked substance, and my prediction that the exchange rate would hit N100 to £1 within a couple of years was met with derision and indignation. They swore blind that even before it could hit

N20 to £1, I would see how the rich Nigerians would bring all their millions back from abroad which would boost demand for the Naira. The logic of why those rich Nigerians would send all the money that they had ensconced abroad back into a currency that was on the slide, under a government driving with no brakes, was lost on me.

The taxi that took me to the chambers of Chief Afe Babalola was typical of the commercial vehicles in Ibadan. It is as if eternal life is ordained for any vehicle once it has been painted in the maroon and yellow drapery of an Ibadan taxi regardless of their physical condition.

The state of repair apart, the cars were impossibly small. These were Nissans and Toyotas that must have been made for home-use-only in the Far East; they were not made for the African physique and certainly not for five full-bodied persons of such species. At 5ft 10 I am not the tallest, yet I so often had to cock my head to one side as I rode in the back of these vehicles to the chambers in the Mokola district of Ibadan. At other times I would be forced to carry my own feet to stay clear of the rain waters that so often forced their way in through the holes in the taxi's under carriage or to provide a manual locking device for the car door by holding the door closed.

The Dancing Lunatic

As with most law chambers in Africa, the head count in Messrs Afe Babalola & Co was modest: a two-partner and ten-staff-practice situated on the first floor of a purpose-built commercial building. Unlike most such chambers, the practice was busy and highly successful. It was the leading law chambers in town.

Chief Afe Babalola, the founder and senior partner, was a man of huge repute, modest stature and a robust smile. Through him I got a close-up insight into the realities of legal practice in Nigeria. Through his files I saw land disputes that had been running for over 20 years and which were no nearer judgment. Through his marble-floored home, I saw the rich rewards and comfortable life style that practice could bring. I saw the reverence with which he was regarded by those who knew him and it was few, indeed, in Ibadan who didn't know him.

In a land where every family dreams of producing a lawyer, the successful lawyer in Nigeria is a super hero that everyone makes it their business to know. It is no wonder that so many of my countrymen have a never-give-up attitude to becoming lawyers however ill-suited they may be for the profession. When you add to it the extreme level of image consciousness that prevails in the country, the colonial trappings of the barristers wig and gown that lawyers in Nigeria are still attached to, and, to top it all, the salutation of "My learned friend", the lawyer status is simply a must-have.

The most remarkable insight of all came from the situation of the Chambers. Unlike in London where barristers and commercial law firms are virtually segregated from the real world, in Nigeria the most successful Chambers can often be found in the heart of humanity itself. The building we were in sat on a corner of the high street in Mokola. On the other corner of the street was a record store.

The fact that this leading law chambers was in such close proximity was of no consequence to the owner of the record shop; he had his own reputation to preserve and his own livelihood to pursue. No lawyer could tell him to keep his speakers within the confines of his shop or get him to reduce the decibel level at which he was blaring the sounds. In truth it was of no consequence to the lawyers, either, because being of a shared culture and language with the record store owner, the music he loved to play was the music we loved to hear. The local madman, it turned out, was equally appreciative.

On one afternoon the speakers had been blaring the heavy bass-line of Eddie Grant's *Hello Africa*. Our mad friend, bare-footed, stark-naked, dust-covered and dread-locked, had obviously heard the call. There he was, on the pavement outside the record store rocking to the sounds as if he had no cares in the world. In that moment he gave new meaning to the expression "raving mad". He danced so well that we all, one by one, including the senior partner, abandoned our work to watch him.

By the end of the show I had a different understanding of insanity in that whilst it may seriously impair some areas of the brain, it could leave other areas totally unaffected if not enhanced. I couldn't imagine that kind of scene being played out on the serene lawns of Lincoln's Inn.

Afe Babalola had given me a chance to show my potential and I had shown it. Had I not read the tea-leaves of the Nigerian economy in the way that I had, and had Esther not been waiting for me in Lagos, I might well have accepted his invitation to stay with the practice and enjoy the occasional entertainment from the dancing lunatic.

I returned to Lagos at the end of the three weeks and, shortly after that, to London as my finances were now very stretched. I had to earn some money before the summer ran out. One consolation of doing security work was that there were always vacancies. ▨

5. AND BACK AGAIN TO LONDON

I had, before heading out to the Law School in Lagos, applied to do a Masters in Law (LLM) at the University of London. My calculation was that the qualification would be technically more challenging than all my previous law studies and so would enable me to demonstrate my potential since I still had not secured even a single interview for pupilage. It had the secondary attraction of staving off the day when I would become one of the most highly educated of Her Majesty's swelling ranks of the unemployed.

The problem with education is that the higher up the qualifications chain you go without finding a way into a related job area, the harder it becomes to persuade any employer to give you a lesser position. You now hear, "sorry, we think you are a little over-qualified for this job" when it seemed only yesterday you were being told that you weren't sufficiently qualified.

The University of London's LLM Programme was run on an inter-collegiate basis. The five principal colleges, Kings College, University College, Queen Mary College, School of African and Oriental Studies and the London School of Economics collaborate to offer a menu of over one hundred law subjects from which you are required to choose four to study in close detail for the year.

I chose Company Law and Business Taxation because I was still hoping against hope that I would, one day, get into Commercial Law practice. My other electives were Carriage of Goods by Sea and Marine Insurance Law. The choice of these last two was ironic because, up to this point in my life, I had never been on a ferry, let alone a ship, and I couldn't tell "starboard" from "port-side". The choice was driven largely by my assessment of the Nigerian economy. That economy being so import-dependent and outward looking, my thinking was that the Law of Carriage of Goods by Sea, and the related area of Marine Insurance Law were critical subjects to have if ever I was going to make the Nigerian experience work for me.

In the meantime, over the summer of 1986, from the 12-hour security shifts that I was doing from Monday to Friday, at sites ranging from investment banks like Morgan-Grenfell, to the NCP Car Park at White City, I managed to save enough money to fly back to Nigeria for the formal call to the Bar ceremony. Again, though it was an occasion of greatest pride for my father, it was my mother who flew down with me for the ceremony.

The call ceremony, and the dinner which preceded it, was a demonstration of the farcical consequences of the colonisation of one group of people by another and the abdication of thought by the colonized about their condition of life.

We were required to wear the full regalia of wig and gown with suits for the call ceremony despite the oppressive heat and the absence of air-conditioning in the over-crowded hall. The ceremony put into clear focus the fact that there are wigs and then there are "wigs".

There were those wigs that had been made in England from traditional horse-hair by Ede & Ravenscroft, and then there were wigs that had been made, in some unknown part of Nigeria, from whatever broom heads the creative genius that manufactured it could lay his hands on. The irony was that the made-in-England wigs, with their luscious white locks, made the daftest sight of all, contrasting, as they did so strongly, with our black faces.

To make matters worse, the school's policy was that this colonial charade must be accompanied by food of the best colonial variety rather than the indigenous stuff. The appetites of Nigerian males being what it is, the upshot was that many were left with stomachs in violent and audible rebellion. An early, and unceremonious, exodus to the local "bukas" was only staved off by the one thing that we Nigerians love more than our food, the opportunity to have our photographs taken.

Esther's call ceremony was the day after mine. Shortly after that I had to return to London and leave her behind. It was on these occasions that I really felt the dislocation in my existence whereby my commercial needs pulled me towards Britain but Nigeria was where I really longed to be.

At that point I really could not say that I had anything to look forward to in Britain. I had no clear path to legal practice, having had rejection after rejection in my applications both to chambers and to the city law firms that I had now extended my appeals to. The experience was made worse by the knowledge that many of my colleagues, who I had helped to understand legal concepts, were now at the point of having completed their pupilage and had started earning.

Further, having spent the last year in Africa, where within the multitude I had enjoyed virtual anonymity, I was returning to a life where I would, once again, stand out to the indigenes as an outsider, however often I myself might lose sight of the reality.

Here then was the dilemma as I stood at the biggest crossroads of my life: I could stay in Nigeria and join the struggle for survival that the honest majority contend with on a daily basis, with little to show for it over the long term, or I could compromise my humanity and go for financial survival in another man's land on another man's terms. Suffice to say that the plane was fully air borne before I had resolved the dilemma and six hours later I was at Gatwick Airport applying to be re-admitted to Brittania, the new Ark that would save the representative few from my part of the world from the rising flood of poverty which was all I could foresee for the majority in my homeland.

I was nevertheless angry about having to confront such a dilemma and the experience stirred some political cells inside my brain. Why could I not enjoy the standard of living that Britain offered in my own land amongst people who looked like me, in the way that English people themselves did? Why could living in another man's land not be for me, as for my English friends, just a matter of choice rather than economic compulsion? Why was Britain and the West generally where it was, and why was Nigeria and Africa in the state that it was?

The LLM course at the LSE made the answer to these questions all the more acute. We had students from all parts of the world, Israel, America, China and beyond. We also had the children of wealthy Nigerians, two of whom, Chuba and Koye, I had met at the Nigerian Law School.

Chuba was Igbo; his uncle was a Justice of the Supreme Court. Koye was Yoruba; his father was one of the most wealthy in southern Nigeria. Through him I got a peek into how the seriously wealthy in Nigeria lived and why the demons that I was struggling with had passed them by. The tennis court in his father's house was better than any that I had played on in London and I was a keen tennis player.

I was, by now, much more politically savvy than I had been during my undergraduate years. It was I who was now forever steering the discussions towards the questions that I needed answered. We spent a lot of lunch hours discussing the politics of Nigeria, the black race and the world. Another military coup having taken place in Nigeria, installing yet another military ruler from the northern part of Nigeria (Ibrahim Babangida), we concluded that the people of southern Nigeria would ultimately have to fight to free themselves from northern domination as we then saw it.

The question then became who would fight. Chuba said the Igbos had fought before in the Biafran war in which the Yorubas had opposed them, and so the Yorubas should fight first. Koye claimed that the Yorubas were too smart for that. Only I, the Yoruba-Briton, was ready to fight but they both laughed me out of the court. So there ended the grand plot to rescue Nigeria that the three of us hatched in the canteen of the LSE. On reflection it is clear that my greater enthusiasm for violent change was borne of the greater hardship that I was enduring as compared with my two compatriots and not just of the air in Britain where people do not put up with oppression for too long.

A job was still no-where in sight and the only way I could get through the LLM year financially was by taking on a forty-hours-a-week security shift at the same time. I was lucky. Securiguard Services Ltd, with whom I had worked over the summer, had taken note of the interest I had expressed in a "one-man-site". As the name suggests, these were sites that required only one security guard. In the course of the assignments I had done while at the Inns of Court School of Law, I had noted that one-man-sites had not only the advantage of saving you from the sometimes trying discussions with the career security guards, they also afforded you the opportunity of studying whilst working.

Law Firms, So Near And Yet So Far

The Almighty, it seemed, had decided to help me to manage my load albeit not to reduce it. I was given a site which was, literally, in the shadows of St. Paul's Cathedral. The top floor of the building was occupied by the London office of the then major, but now defunct, U.S. law firm, Coudert Brothers.

According to their brochure the firm had been established in downtown Manhattan in 1853 and had grown into a global institution. They were the first U.S. law firm to establish a presence in Paris in 1879, London in 1960 and China in 1979. This was major league law and it didn't matter that I was only their security guard. It was the first law firm in the U.K. that I had ever set foot in. At the weekends I had the chance to sit in the partner's luxurious offices, hold imaginary meetings in their main conference room and generally fantasize about my future life.

The hours were four each night from Monday to Friday, 6p.m. to 10p.m., and ten hours each day on Saturday and Sunday, from 8a.m. to 6p.m. St. Paul was my timekeeper and the bells of his cathedral would always toll to let me know how much more of my time I had to spend in confinement each day.

Although every day from Monday to Sunday was thus long for me, yet in my circumstances I could not be more grateful. The site was really tailor made. It was a mere three bus stops from the LSE at the Strand, and there were a good number of buses that I could leap on to as I rushed out from lectures or the canteen. When the cathedral announced my release at 10p.m., I would stand on its steps to wait for the Bus 141 to take me home to Newington Green where I was then still living with my parents.

Weekends were the hardest. It wasn't just because of the longer ten hour shifts but more to do with the fact that you hardly saw anyone else, except the odd tourist straying past the side-street: it really did amount to solitary confinement. It was only on the odd occasion that any of the staff in the offices came in at the weekend and when they did they didn't break the silence for very long.

Harder still was the impact on my social life. I was twenty-four and should have been in the prime of my social existence. Parties and clubs are hard to enjoy on Friday and Saturday nights when you have to wake up by 6.30a.m. the following morning. The football that I should have been playing on Saturdays and Sundays, to make up for the time that I lost under my father's iron rule in my adolescent years, also had to be sacrificed.

Many a time, as I stood alone on the steps of St. Paul's Cathedral, I would look up at the cathedral, and beyond, and ask why my lot in life had to be so much harder than that of anyone that I knew. No answer ever came back, at least so I thought at the time. However that was because my church up-bringing had led me to expect that a dialogue with the Maker would be like a telephone conversation: dynamic and personal.

It is only in more recent years that I have come to understand that God answers our questions by revelation only and that the fullness of the answers that you receive are dictated by the extent to which your inner eye is open. Through this appreciation, I came to realize that if my life hadn't followed the course that it did, I would not have this story to tell.

One of the partners at Coudert Brothers took sufficient note of my daily head-down posture behind the security desk to ask what it was I was reading. He was genuinely surprised and impressed when I told him I was doing an LLM in Commercial Law at the LSE. Looking back I can understand how surreal the sight must have been to him, but then he didn't live in my world.

I didn't have sufficient presence of mind at that time to ask him if he would mind taking a look at my CV in case he knew of anyone who might be interested. I had discounted the possibility of getting in with his firm because I knew they only practiced U.S. law. I was also mindful of the fact that a transition from being the firm's doorman to one of its legal team would be too dramatic to be taken seriously.

He did, however, do me one kindness without my even asking. He got the approval of his partners to my using their law library. I thanked him profusely. That I had been using their library all along anyway was beside the point. After this episode, the head of the London operations, who had previously been oblivious to my existence, now afforded me an un-smiling nod as he left each evening.

The LLM programme was disappointing for being conceptually no more stretching than all the other law exams had been. Though the syllabus was deeper, the exams were just another test of memory. I couldn't see how it was going to set me apart from other runners. The saving grace was the smaller tutorial groups which allowed for more discussion and analysis. Through these I managed to make an impression on the lecturers, especially Professor Aubrey Diamond (Carriage of Goods by Sea) and Mrs Judith Freedman (Business Tax).

Earlier in the summer I had done a security assignment in Basinghall Street. I did not, at that time, know that a number of the firms that I had been fruitlessly applying to were round the corner from the site. Slaughter & May were just up the road and Linklaters & Paine were round the corner near the Guildhall. This was a particularly difficult one-man-site. It was a twelve-hour night shift on Saturdays and Sundays. The only consolation was that it was better than being part of the crew at the Prudential or at the Barbican Theatre or worst of all, patrolling the ghostly, creaky floors in the Directors' rooms at Morgan Grenfell in Moorgate.

It was while at Basinghall Street that I became quite creative in performing my duties. The security desk was directly in front of the glass doors at the entrance to the building. It was impossible to sleep there and to ensure that you didn't sleep at all you were required to make "check-in" calls to the control office every forty-five minutes. I got round the location problem by crashing out in the side room. The chairs were not conducive as they had arm-rests, but I would line four of them up and slot myself under the arms. The solution to the forty-five-minute check-in calls was an alarm clock set to ring on the forty-minute mark. So it happened on each shift that after I had tired of reading, I would snatch moments of unauthorised sleep.

It was at this site that I came across copies of 'Taxation', the Institute of Taxation's magazine. I was good at tax law and I was impressed by the salaries that tax jobs appeared to command.

Inspired by the magazine, in an uncharacteristic move, I decide to discuss the problem I was having with Mrs Judith Freedman, my Tax Law lecturer. Someone had told me that she was once a tax partner at Freshfields. She listened with compassion but explained that she had no strings to pull. She did, however, advise that I extend my applications to large accountancy practices as they were known to recruit barristers.

For the first time a light had been shone on my pathway to legal practice. It was only a flickering candle light, but in the gloomy darkness that I had been walking in since my graduation in 1984, it was blinding.

We were nearly at the end of the LLM programme and there was little time to waste, there being no more studies behind which I could take refuge from the shame of being considered unemployable. I needed a job and needed it quickly.

With an updated CV in hand, I went to see some recruitment agencies that specialised in supplying staff for accountants. In desperation I also started sending my CV to criminal law chambers. Gone was my insistence on commercial or chancery practice. I needed a job damn it and any job would do.

A Life of Crime or Commerce

It was the summer of 1987 and I had graduated three years previously in the summer of 1984. In the intervening period I had lost count of how many applications I had sent out and the many different ways I had worded my covering letter to persuade the reader to give me an interview. Again and again I found my route to the more suitable jobs blocked by quantitative reasoning tests that tested a process of reasoning that had no obvious relationship or relevance to legal reasoning. Lacking the reasoning technique to overcome these tests, I never got to the stage of being tested on my legal reasoning. It seemed to me then a strange way of identifying the best lawyers.

Then for the first time in my life, and in the same week, I received two offers for interview.

The first came from a Criminal Law chambers in Inner Temple. At last someone on the inside of the profession had opened the door just a crack to take a look at me. The second came a day or so later via the recruitment consultants, Accountancy Personnel. It was an offer of interview with the largest firm of Chartered Accountants, Coopers & Lybrand (now Price Waterhouse Coopers), with a view to joining their Employee Share Schemes Unit.

With all the letters of regret that I had received from all other applications that I had made, I knew that my future depended on these two interviews. The interview at the barrister's chambers came first. I arrived in good time and took a seat in the reception just outside the interview room. The chambers was just like any other barrister's chambers in the eighties, with wood flooring and dark oak paneling. A number of us were being interviewed for the pupilage post and on my arrival I sat next to one of my fellow contestants. After no more than ten minutes he was on the way out and I was on the way in.

The barrister conducting the interview made an attempt at my name which I barely recognised. I corrected him, "Ogun-etim-oju" I said. As if in a hurry to move on to firmer ground, he proceeded to ask why I had chosen to read law and whether there were any lawyers in my family. I told him about my father's aspirations for himself and how I inherited the mantle of a wannabe lawyer. I was expecting some technical questions but they never came. The next thing I knew was that the fellow was thanking me for attending and assuring me that he would be writing to me shortly. So brief was the encounter that I really didn't know whether I had performed well or badly.

The interview at Coopers & Lybrand was the following week. Mrs Shonubi (my host at the Nigerian Law School) was staying with us for the summer. She knew a lot more than I did about the standing of Coopers & Lybrand in the world at that time.

"You have arrived", she declared. I haven't had the interview yet, I thought.

Her excitement did, however, rub off on me. The interview was on Monday morning. On the Sunday night, on the way back from my security post, I decided to pay a reconnaissance visit to Plumtree Court, the firm's then headquarters and the venue for the Monday morning encounter.

As I turned into Plumtree Court, there was this magnificent white building with beautiful arches set in lush green foliage lit up by strategically positioned external lighting. No wonder Mrs Shonubi had been so excited, I thought. This was a building far removed from the austere surroundings of the Inner Temple Chambers and much closer to some of those offices I had been working in as a security guard all these years and which had fed my dreams as to how my future office would look. As I stood there in the night sky looking up at the building, I knew that I had to get this job. I lingered a few moments in silent prayer.

The following morning I was there in good time. The visit the night before had been helpful not only in getting my timing right but also in getting me into the right mental state. As I sat in the reception and looked out through the glass frontage into the rich foliage in the courtyard, I became ever more convinced that this was the place that those who knew me had to associate me with as compared with the Criminal Bar. The impression it gave me was that you had to be good to get in here and that impression was confirmed by all the sharp looking people that were reporting for work.

I was still indulging my thoughts when Ms Belinda Bridgen's secretary appeared by my side and uttered my name with the hesitation reflecting the difficulty that she was having pronouncing it. "Yes, that's me", I replied whilst thinking to myself: as if it could be any one else here.

Belinda was a partner within the corporate tax practice. She was a woman in a man's world but she was their equal in every respect. Her conduct was as masculine as any, from her chain-smoking down to her use of expletives. In the interview, however, she was charming. We struck a rapport very quickly. I had put her at ease over my name right at the outset by explaining that friends and family reduced the Akindele to "Dele" and the Ogunetimoju to "Ogun" and for now at least she could consider herself a friend. The ice was broken, her laughter bellowed and the job was mine.

Even then I could not believe it when the letter came. I knew the letter was from her because the white, high quality envelope bore the franking mark of Coopers & Lybrand. I knew it was a job offer because it came in a large envelope and I had come to associate small, thin envelopes with letters of rejection.

There it was. I was being offered a job in the Employee Share Schemes Unit of Coopers & Lybrand, the premier firm of accountants in the United Kingdom and a global institution. At long last I was being let into corporate Britain at A Level that required me to use my education and my mind. The Ogunetimojus, after a long and arduous journey all the way from Nigeria had got their toes in the doorway of Corporate Britain at last.

When the offer of pupilage in the criminal chambers came a day or so later my mind had already been made up. If I was going to climb Mount Everest (for that is how the barricades surrounding legal practice in England appeared to me) I was going to do it through the North Face of commercial law that few blacks had scaled rather than the well worn track of criminal law. Besides, the black community in Britain and beyond needed some of their sons to understand City speak and the language of high commerce.

An Introduction to the World of Finance
The £12,500 salary that Coopers were starting me on then read to me like a fortune from where I was coming from and had the added attraction that I would be working in the field of high commerce.

The alternative as an unpaid pupil barrister in criminal law practice would have meant more struggle, debt and security assignments to keep body and soul together. It was quite simply a no-brainer for me. I then proceeded to write the only letter that I have ever written in my life to decline a job offer. For one who had made so many unsuccessful job applications, it was a strange feeling sending that letter.

The team that I was in at Coopers had a few others who had been called to the English Bar and who, for one reason or another, had bailed out. This left many of them with huge ego problems aggravated by being regarded by the Accountants as being not quite their equals.

The biggest amongst them, in every sense of the word, was one Owain Franks. He was at that time a Senior Manager and on a power-play to becoming the highest that a non-accountant could be, a Director. Complete with braces to hold up his generous stomach he loved the sensation of darting from meeting to meeting. He seemed to find it difficult to relate to the male members of his team, perhaps because they didn't show quite the same reverence for his capability as a lawyer. Owain's outlook was simple. You either gushed over him and so were "with him", or you didn't and he didn't recognise you.

His greatest fan was Nicola who graduated the year before me at the London Metropolitan University and had joined Coopers immediately after the Bar. She had always had a knack for parleying with those in authority. It was she who I had glimpsed sitting on the desk of the Head of the Law Department in casual conversation with him as if they were colleagues. I had viewed it at the time as audacious but I came to learn that in western culture, competence commands more respect than age.

This cultural lesson was underlined for me when Nicola, being a grade above me in the hierarchy, asked me to go and collect a file for her. When she made the request my Nigerian instincts, where age, titles and qualifications ranked ahead of everything else, were first to the fore: this one, I thought to myself, who, but for the year I took off from studies after my A Levels, would have been my contemporary and whose honours degree was A Level below mine, and who didn't have an LLM to boast of let alone the status as a barrister in another jurisdiction, asking me to go and collect a file for her! All the same, I had to swallow my pride and get the file she requested. This was England, not Nigeria.

John Shoebridge was the other Senior Manager. He could not have been more different. He was not a lawyer but his legal reasoning was way ahead of the lawyers. He was a gentleman of advancing years who had been recruited from the highest ranks of the Inland Revenue Technical Division. The accountants had developed the practice of going after civil servants like John who had previously been operating as gamekeepers, and who, having taken early retirement on maximum pension packages from the Inland Revenue, were now open to spending their twilight years enjoying the higher remuneration levels that the private sector offered.

John had been one of the best in the Technical Division, and it showed. He knew the intricacies of the Share Scheme legislation inside out. He was the master of the written word and I had the good fortune to be working under him.

Before I started at Coopers my letter writing was fairly good but he showed me the higher level although, to begin with, the exercise was very bruising to my confidence. Every letter I submitted to him for review came back almost completely re-written, however hard I tried.

The feeling of inadequacy was only made worse by the fact that when I read his re-worked version, I could see that his read so much more simply and fluidly. Like a loving father putting his son through the hoops over and over again, however much the son hated it, he sensed my frustration but refused to lower the standards that he was expecting of me. There was a tell-tale glint in his eye the day he approved a three-page advice letter that I had compiled without a single alteration. The adopted son had come of age in the art of letter writing.

Clive Tulloch was the partner in charge of the department within which the Share Scheme Unit was contained. With a long sharp nose, an almost lipless mouth, and Etonian and Oxbridge mannerisms, he was the caricature of the English Mandarin. Looking back, it was as well that the more brusque Belinda Bridgen had conducted my interview as I never managed to gel with Clive. Come to think of it, it was probably because of his very appearance that candidates were spared the encounter.

The Share Ownership Revolution
Employee Share Schemes were a critical part of Margaret Thatcher's

capitalist revolution to break the chains and bonds that the socialists had wrapped the British economy up in. Her party's campaign slogan, "Britain isn't working" in which countless unemployed were depicted queuing for work, was more than just a slogan: for her it was an item of faith that all the levers of government had to be used to turn the Ark Brittania around from the economic iceberg to which she was heading.

The first stage of the revolution was to break the hold of the trade unions, principal amongst which was Arthur Scargill's National Union of Miners. These large unions had shown again and again that though it was the government of the day that had its foot on the accelerator of the economy, it was they who controlled the brakes: once Arthur and his men gave the signal the whole juggernaut could be brought to a halt. Like the Boudicca that she was, Mrs Thatcher dedicated her first term in office to this the biggest battle.

Taking her inspiration from the example of Prime Minster Lee Kuan Yew of Singapore, she introduced laws that made it unlawful for union leaders to call strikes without a referendum of the members and which outlawed "flying pickets"– the practice whereby persons who were not employed in the establishment in question joined or formed a line of protest outside the place of work to dissuade or prevent the workers from going to work.

Having used the law as a stick to break the back of the once all-powerful trade unions, the stage was set for Mrs Thatcher to use the law as a carrot to lay the foundations for the second stage of the British economic revolution.

Again borrowing from Singapore's Lee Kuan Yew, the philosophy underlying the second phase was that "private ownership is good". State-owned enterprises like British Airways, British Petroleum and British Steel were sold into private ownership as part of the biggest privatisation programme the world had yet seen. The full forces of capitalism were being unleashed.

Public resistance to the programme that might have been expected was virtually non-existent. This was partly the result of the prior emasculation of the trade unions who would have been expected to lead the protests. Just as significant were the pay-offs offered to the public by way of opportunities to buy shares in the newly privatised companies at generous discounts. It was the original National Lottery where everyone was guaranteed to be a winner. The third phase was tax cuts for owners and tax incentive schemes for employees known as Employee Share Schemes.

The strategic objective of the Thatcher Government was to shift the loyalty of workers from their unions to their employers by getting them to think like owners and the only way to make them think like owners was to make them owners even if their ownership was limited to a modest part of the whole. Since most enterprises were established as companies owned through shareholdings, this called for schemes that would allow employees to own shares in their employing companies.

The schemes were already in extensive use in that citadel of capitalism, the U.S. and the Thatcher Government simply imported the development. Since ownership necessarily involves some degree of risk to which most who choose to be employees are adverse, the offer of the chance to become owners needed some sugar-coating.

The sugar-coat took the form of tax savings attaching to the shares such that when the shares were sold, the difference between the price that the employee paid for the shares and the price he received for them on selling the shares was, potentially, tax-free. At a time when the top rate of tax was forty percent this was a very attractive incentive indeed and it compared, very favourably, with the amount of regular salary that the same employee would need to receive to produce the same amount of after-tax income.

The schemes that attracted these official tax breaks were known as approved schemes. The rules of the scheme had to comply with the detailed conditions laid out in the legislation and, also, had to be certified by the Technical Division of the Inland Revenue as being so compliant.

As surely as day follows night, because of the imperfection of human language, whenever government drafts laws to open the door to a defined point, some smart-arsed people will start looking for ways to make money by pushing the door wider. To safeguard the public revenue, the government needed equally sharp minds to police the boundaries that it had set in the legislation. The Technical Division of the Inland Revenue was that unit. Their job was to critically review the share schemes that were submitted for approval to ensure they were within the limits laid down by the law. Schemes that were approved attracted tax relief; schemes that were unapproved did not.

There were three kinds of approved share schemes: the Profit

Sharing Scheme, the Savings Related Share Option Scheme and, the king of them all, the Executive Share Option Scheme.

The Profit Sharing and Savings Related Schemes were the burnt offerings to the socialist spirit in that all employees had to be allowed to participate on an equal footing. It was the Executive Share Option Scheme that unleashed the true spirit of capitalism. Under this scheme the top boys could grant themselves the right to buy shares in the companies for which they worked at today's market value on a bet that the value of the shares would rise. It was a gamble but it was the kind of gamble that everyone likes – the kind where you can't lose.

You couldn't lose on the bet because you didn't have to pay your stake (the market value of the shares at the date the option was granted to you) until such time as you were satisfied that the value of the shares was sufficiently higher than the stake price. For so long as the value of the shares was lower than the stake price (in industry-speak "the shares were underwater") you kept your powder dry and simply didn't exercise your right. Obviously once you made the call and exercised your option to buy, you now carried the same risk as any other shareholder and the value of your investment could go up as well as down.

Shares acquired through an approved share scheme enjoyed a special icing on the cake with the compliments of HM Treasury. The icing was that provided the scheme was an approved scheme and the shares were acquired in accordance with the scheme rules, all the growth between the market value of the shares at the date the option was granted to you (your stake) and the market value of the shares at the date you exercised your option to buy them at that original value, was tax free.

At a time when the top rate of tax was 40 percent, this was very sweet icing indeed. Besides that, with a good tax adviser, there was significant scope to avoid tax on the growth in the market value of the shares from the date you bought the shares up until the date you sold them.

The fiction on the back of which the schemes were accorded these tax breaks was that by incentivizing the captains of the ship, the crew would be assured of a safer passage and a swifter journey, and the ship and cargo owners alike would be enriched and the country, as a whole, would be all the happier.

The reality was that the success of the voyage turned much more on the elements over which the captains had little or no control e.g. a favourable wind. In a "bull market" share values are pulled up across the board regardless of any value added by the top guns. Likewise in a "bear market" share values are pulled down despite the best efforts of the management team.

The political philosophy underlying the scheme was to get management on the same side as the owners and to pull them away from the rank and file workers.

A scheme offering such tax-sweetened rewards to the select few and based on such an ideology had to have some limits and conditions built into it. The limit on participation was that the maximum value of the shares over which the executive could hold options was four times his annual remuneration not exceeding £100,000.00 per annum. So a real top gun could have a stake of up to £400,000.00. The conditions were that the options had to have been held for at least three years before they could be exercised and there had to be a six month gap between each exercise.

In recognition of the fact that there would be some businesses that could not or else, did not wish to, offer share participation to their employees, the legislation also provided for cash-based schemes. The Profit Related Pay Scheme was a tax-sweetened scheme that gave employers an opportunity to pay staff cash bonuses that were directly tied to their year-on-year growth in profits. Again to guard against the tax breaks being stretched beyond the pre-set parameters, the legislation was tightly drafted and carefully policed.

Employers wishing to take advantage of the array of employee incentive schemes that were available needed expert advice to draw up the scheme rules in a way that was not only compliant with applicable legislation but was also consistent with their commercial objectives: just as the revenue were concerned not to give more tax breaks than they intended, the employers were equally keen not to give more to their employees than had been budgeted for.

The share-scheme lawyer needed a broad range of skills: the ability to make sense of tightly-drafted legislation and the limited body of applicable case law; the ability to draft a coherent and compliant set of scheme rules; the ability to integrate the rights conferred by the schemes on the employees into the employment relationship so that they gave rise to rights only in accordance with the wishes of the employer; the ability to draft all the necessary ancillary legal documents from amendments to Articles of Association, variations in share capital, Board and Company Resolutions and trust deeds.

These skill sets were the natural preserve of lawyers but the accountants had stolen a march on the law firms. This was largely because as the auditors of company finances they get an early insight into the company's financial performance and growth plans. However it was also because the tax department within law firms was historically seen as a support function for the other departments rather then as a potential profit centre in its own right.

For me it was a fortunate circumstance that the accountants had made this niche theirs. They needed lawyers to consolidate their advantage and, in the position that I was in, on the outside of the inside of legal practice in England, I was only too willing to assist.

Three years later, however, the excitement of working at Coopers was gone. John Shoebridge had retired. His replacement, Sid Singh, a technically brilliant, though slightly dogmatic man from the Indian Ocean island of Goa, had become a friend of mine but the petty politics within the share schemes unit was getting worse not better.

Besides, having opted out of doing tax compliance work and with the very tough Institute of Tax (ATII) exams which Coopers required me to take causing me some unfamiliar embarrassment, I sensed slow moving traffic ahead on the career path with the accountants.

My protest that I had been recruited to produce top quality legal work and that tax returns and passing the ATII Finals had no bearing on this, fell on deaf ears. The experience drove home the fact that I was still a fish out of water and that I would not get best value from my abilities until I found my way into the legal profession. It was time to pack my bags and get back on the road to find a way into commercial law practice in England.

The omens looked promising. According to the recruitment agents, the law firms were playing catch up with the accountants in the highly lucrative field of employee share schemes and they were desperate for lawyers with share schemes experience from the leading accounting practices. Could my share schemes experience be the Trojan horse that would get me behind the fortress walls of the legal profession? ▓

6. A ROSE
BY ANY
OTHER NAME ...

It was a lunch time visit that I paid to Quarry Dougall's offices at High Holborn to submit my CV which was now competitive on any objective measure. Respectable O Levels and A Levels, Head Boy, Upper Second Class Honours, Barrister, LLM and now, most crucially, three years experience with the No.1 firm of Chartered Accountants, Coopers & Lybrand.

Stephen Rodney, the consultant, was particularly enthusiastic. "We'll have no problems placing you", he declared. I left him to re-work the CV into Quarry Dougall's house style and to send it out to the law firms on his books. Then we waited. And we waited.

After an indecent amount of time had passed it was clear that there was no interest. My heart sank once more.

What does a man like me have to do to get into legal practice in this country, I thought. I knew it wasn't a question of ability because so many that I knew with less ability were already in practice.

There was something about my CV in particular that these law firms clearly didn't like. I knew it wasn't the fact that I had attended an inner London comprehensive and a polytechnic because I knew of others who had similar unconventional credentials who were already in. I just couldn't place my finger on the problem. It was looking increasingly as if, like my father before me, I was going to end up just another frustrated would-be lawyer.

Luckily I didn't have to solve the riddle by myself. Stephen Rodney was also baffled as to why none of the law firms were interested.

"I know these jobs are there" he said earnestly. *"It's my job to know who is still looking and when the post has been filled".*

Before I could offer any comment he declared: *"you know what? I think it's your name"*.

"What do you mean?" I said.

He continued: *"I think it is the 'Akindele Ogunetimoju'. If you don't mind, I will take your name off the CV and send it back out."*

"Stephen", I said, *"I don't care what you do, I just need to practice law."*

And so the CV was sent out again. It was the CV of the would-be-lawyer formerly known as Akindele Ogunetimoju but who now had no name.

There was nothing unusual about a recruitment consultant sending a CV out with no name because they have to protect the confidence of those who are looking to change jobs or else employees would be wary of risking the bird in hand for the one in the bush. The de-personalised CV is the perfect tool in these circumstances. It gives the prospective employer everything he needs to know about the candidate bar his identity. In place of the name the prospective employer is given a candidate number until such time has he indicates that he wants to interview the candidate.

The other protective tool is the use by the agent himself of a code name whenever he calls the candidate at his current place of work. A week later, Stephen called using his code name.

"You won't believe it", he said. *"They are interested"*.

I was still in stupor when he added: *"You could sue them for a lot of money you know, coz this is disgraceful"*.

I said: *"Stephen I don't want their money, it's just their experience I need."*

While Stephen was arranging the interview, I had a chance to reflect. I thought back to the education I had received in England since coming to the country at the age of seven and three quarters, not speaking a word of English. I reflected on how, in the quest for a good education in order to get a good job, I had virtually lost my native Yoruba language: I had traded in a life in my own land with my relations and people for a life in another man's land where I had committed myself fully to adjusting to their moral code, their humour and general outlook on life in a bid to fit in and get on. I had made all these sacrifices and worked hard at putting myself in shape in all respects only to find myself denied the anticipated rewards because I was holding to that last reminder of who I really was, my name.

It was a bitter pill to swallow when I thought of all those applications that I had made over the years, and of all those letters of rejection which had left me questioning my abilities and which had so undermined my self-belief. It wasn't just the jobs I had applied for since graduation. Never being of the work-shy type, and having collected 100 percent attendance certificates in every year of secondary school, I had applied for all manner of jobs during school holidays. Again and again I found that it was only the jobs like security work that no one else wanted that would be open to me. Yet swallow the pill I had to.

I absorbed the lessons whole-heartedly. I came to understand why it was that black-Caribbeans with their British names were better represented in British society than their black-African counterparts. I came, also, to understand why Jewish immigrants like Robert Maxwell had changed their names to hide their identity. I was proud of my name. "Akindele" means the strong/brave one has arrived. "Ogunetimoju" means the god of war never embarrasses me. In England it meant only that you did not belong.

The lesson having been learnt the hard way that England is not America and that your name as much as your race can seriously affect your destiny, I came to two conclusions. First, I could not make the complete surrender of my integrity and identity that success in Britain required of an outsider like me. Secondly, having taken this stance, I knew that I had to think beyond the forthcoming interviews. I promised myself that this would be the last time that I would allow myself to be dependent on others for my livelihood and sense of worth.

There and then the resolve to establish my own law firm formed. Thus it was that before I had even attended the interviews with the City law firms I had worked out my exit strategy. Partnership was not going to be for me: if I had had such difficulty getting into practice, I was not going to deceive myself into thinking that staying in these firms over the longer term was going to be any less fraught with considerations outside my control. Thus my plan was to get in and grab as much experience as I could and set up my own law firm at the earliest possible opportunity.

Ever since I read how Jesus Christ on the cross cried out: "My God, My God, why hast thou forsaken me?" and received no answer back, God, for me, has communicated with man through revelation rather than dialogue and it is at the moments of our greatest trials that we have the greatest capacity to perceive His guidance. Thus it is that the dusk of our greatest challenges is the dawn of our greatest achievements. It is when the full scale of a problem or challenge becomes clear that the path to over-come it is also revealed. Until then every solution is half-baked and potentially misconceived.

The other insight was the importance of looking at an issue through the other person's periscope. My father had told me about the problems that his generation had had finding accommodation when they first came to England. My generation was now looking to join the professions and law was the most conservative of them all. It occurred to me that it wasn't just a matter of the sentiments of the members of the legal profession but of the clients that they served.

Though social Britain may lay claim to being multi-cultural, the world of business in Britain is very much a white world and the commercial law firms were in business to serve that customer base. Since theirs was not a social enterprise, how would the recruitment of a black lawyer serve their business agenda if equally qualified white lawyers were available when the white lawyers were more likely to have connections within the business community that could produce work? Thus it became clear to me that technical excellence alone was not sufficient in a business like law that revolved around personal relationships.

I also came to understand why it was that members of the Caribbean community, although facing the same colour bar, had a better track record of overcoming this hurdle. The English names that they had inherited through their forebears' trauma in the slave trade enabled them, on the face of the CV, at least, to pass themselves off as sons of the soil. My experience showed that once by fair means or foul the black candidate can make it through to the interview and perform competently at the interview, only the die-hards will keep the door locked.

Mr Ogun I Presume

The first interview was with Allen & Overy. This was major league law, the level I was meant to perform at. This time I was going in, not as a security guard, as at Coudert Bothers, but as a prospective member of their team of high performance lawyers.

As the day of the interview approached, Stephen called: *"What name should we give them; they are asking for a name"*.

We both saw the funny side of the situation; it was our little private joke.

"Leave it with me to think about it".

My first thought was to push the joke further. It was England's greatest story teller, Shakespeare who wrote:

"What is in a name? A rose by any other name would smell as sweet". Tempting as it was, I resisted using *"Mr Romeo".*

My strategy was going to be non-confrontational and I didn't want to have to explain too much. In the end, I decided to go with my real name but the less formal version of it as I had given Belinda Bridgen at Coopers & Lybrand.

Most Yoruba names are reduceable into integral parts. Thus from the first name, *Akindele,* you can get *Akin*, which is what my Grandmother always called me, or you can take *Dele* which is what my parents called me at home. From the *Ogunetimoju* you got *Ogun* which is how my father was affectionately addressed by his contemporaries.

The strategy was to anglicize this African name as much as possible so as not to give the game away ahead of the interview. I called Stephen back to say:

"Tell them to expect Mr D. Ogun"

That "Mr Ogun" did not exactly suggest a candidate from Stratford-upon-Avon did not matter; it was sufficient that it did not obviously point to Equatorial Africa.

No.1 St Paul's Churchyard was an address that struck a chord with me when I saw it. It was literally on the other side of the steps of St Paul's Cathedral where I had stood after my security assignments waiting for the bus home. It was a building that I looked at each day from the upper deck of Bus 141 on my way to and from my security post at Coudert Brothers' offices without ever realizing that these were the offices of Allen & Overy. In vintage English style it was a presence that was not proclaimed very loudly – just a small brass plate by the door.

"A miracle. So all this while St. Paul had in fact been passing on my lament and the Divine One had the answer on the other side of the Cathedral", I thought.

The day of the encounter came and I was shown up to the reception by the security man. The décor in the reception said "This is England". The chairs were traditional as was the antique sideboard and the Axminster carpet. Tea was served in the best of English bone-china tea sets with a selection of the best quality English biscuits.

A very English looking mature gentleman, in a bespoke English suit came to collect me from the reception. I watched his eyes as he enquired:

"*Mr Ogun?*" which we pronounced as "O'gun" with the emphasis on the "gun".

"*Yes, that's me*" I responded, as I stood to take his extended hand.

The eyes betrayed some embarassment, but it was only for an instant. We exchanged polite conversation as we headed towards one of the conference rooms. He introduced himself as the partner in charge of the personal tax team and explained why they were looking to bolster the team with someone of my kind of experience.

The interview went very well. There was no laughter (he just wasn't that kind of man) but there was a genuine connection. When it came to my turn to ask the questions I asked whether there would be opportunities for me to use the corporate tax knowledge that I had acquired on the LLM course. Allen & Overy, he explained, had separate departments for Personal Tax and Corporate Tax and the post I was being interviewed for was within the Personal Tax Department.

It wasn't the answer I wanted but since my objective was to get in by all possible means I made noises to suggest it was of no great consequence even though it really was. I regarded myself as an all-rounder in law and I was all too aware of the danger of becoming over-specialized. This was in fact what was driving my need to move on from Coopers & Lybrand. While it would have been a great leap forward to move from share schemes in a "Big Five" accountancy firm to the same discipline in a "magic circle" law firm, my real strategic objective was to use the share schemes experience as my Trojan horse to get into mainstream commercial law. The interview ended and he said they would be writing to me.

The second interview was at Lovells or Lovell White Durrant, as it then was. Only the Holborn viaduct stood between Lovells offices and Coopers & Lybrand's offices at Plumtree Court. Even so, throughout the three years that I had been with Coopers, it was only the once that the presence of the law firm had registered with me. The occasion was when we had to send a package to Coopers

& Lybrand's Hong Kong office and I had been instructed by Owain Franks to take the package to Lovells post room in order to catch their post to their Hong Kong offices. So, once again, I knew exactly where I was going when the day of the interview came.

The Lovells reception at 65 Holborn Viaduct told a different story from Allen & Overy's. While Allen & Overy looked to tradition, Lovells spoke of the future. The light-oak parquet flooring worked well with the ruby-red rugs, the floor-to-ceiling glass surround and the brightly lit suspended ceiling. The receptionists were uniformly smart and pleasing on the eye.

I had been told to ask for Mr Chris Major. I sat on one of the leather sofas facing towards the entrance to the reception area and the receptionist's desk. After a short interval the doors to the reception area swung open and Chris Major breezed in. He had an almost Mediterranean complexion, an emerging belly and a light bounce in his step. His suit was well tailored but not bespoke.

I heard him ask the receptionist to identify Mr Ogun. I stood up to meet with him even as the receptionist was gesturing in my direction. Once again I looked at his eyes to see if they betrayed anything about the CV of Akindele Ogunetimoju that had not found favour before. There was nothing of that nature.

We settled into the interview quickly and the laughter on both sides was not long in coming. Something told me that Chris was going to be another paternal figure for me as John Shoebridge had been at Coopers.

In the course of the interview we were joined by Anthony Davies, one of the other partners in the Tax Department.

As far as first impressions went, he was very much of the same stock as the partner at Allen & Overy had been. The suit was very much bespoke and the shoes were best English "Church's" (one of the handmade shoes of preference of the English nobility). It turned out that he was a product of Eton and Oxford. Interviews are all about chemistry and I was only relieved that Chris Major was taking the interview and that Anthony had only popped in to have a look. Soon afterwards he left Chris to carry on with it.

When it came to my turn to ask questions, I asked the same question as I had asked at the Allen & Overy interview about the scope to use the corporate tax education that I had received. When the reply was affirmative, I become even more enthusiastic about joining Lovells.

I wasn't to know at that time that Chris shared the enthusiasm. Not that he hadn't given me what, in retrospect, was a clear signal, but, with the difficulties that I had experienced in my journey to law, my senses had become numbed to anything that suggested a "Yes".

"Are you seeing anyone else"? he had asked.

"I am waiting to hear back from Allen & Overy" was my answer.

"Make sure you speak to me before you go anywhere else" he said. *"You should hear from us within a few days".*

Stephen Rodney called on the afternoon of the interview:

"How did it go"?

"It went very well. I liked the bloke; I hope they give me a chance", I said.

Two days later Stephen called again using his code name:

"Congratulations!", He said. *"I've just heard back from Lovells and they are asking how much you want".*

My ears rang with the news. I was floating. I barely heard him as he explained what they meant by "how much do you want". He later explained that I was being presented with three salary options: A lower starting figure with an increase after three months; a higher starting figure with an increase after six months or the highest figure with an increase in a year.

I decided to play it down the middle as I didn't want to give the impression of being too money-focused by demanding the highest starting figure on offer; neither did I want to show my desperation by going for the humblest figure. As it happened the £31,000 which was the middle figure, as at December, 1990, represented real money to me, it was a clear £10,000 per annum more than what I was earning at Coopers.

The money of course wasn't the issue. What mattered was that six years after completing my law degree and five years after being called to the English Bar, I had arrived at last, in major league law; the level where, ever since the early days at London Metropolitan University when I had discovered my hidden talent for the law, I felt I belonged but which I knew not how I was going to get to.

That afternoon my head was in a complete whirl. Bad news I had learnt to handle; not so with news that was good as I had little experience of handling such news.

The Coopers office at Plumtree Court was set out over a rectangular formation around an inner atrium. My concentration had gone and I needed desperately to clear my head. I took a walk around the first floor block and then joined a lift to continue my circumnavigation on the second floor. All the while my mind alternated from anger at the final proof that it was my name that had kept me out of my law career for so long, back to relief and elation that, at long last, someone had agreed to unbolt the door to the profession and to let me in.

Now I am a City Lawyer!

The large white richly embossed envelope from Lovells arrived the next day with the formal offer of employment with Group F5 (the F stood for financial) as a "Corporate Tax Lawyer". The words read as music to my ears. I had long fantasized about the title: "Corporate Tax Lawyer". First, because corporate law is regarded as a class above all other areas of law (if only because that is where the big money deals are); and further because tax law is the area of law that is perceived to be the most intellectually challenging. The corporate tax lawyer therefore commands the ultimate respect.

Perhaps as a consequence of the extreme intellectual rigours of the discipline, the tax department in any law firm tends to contain the quirkiest of characters. Lovells tax department was no exception. The quirkiest of all by a long margin was my roommate Adrian Brettel. His trademarks were Hush Puppies, and ties that were chosen to offend the senses in size, colour and design and suits with sleeves that overshot his arms by a consistent three inches. He spoke with a slightly affected stammer but he had the purest of hearts. His life was law, tax law in particular, and his "Mama".

Adrian was a formidable tax lawyer: a walking encyclopaedia in the discipline. A product of Oxford, he could call up tax legislation, tax cases and authorities at an instant from memory. If ever you were at a loss to find learning on a tax issue you had only to ask Adrian and he would immediately make the quest his personal mission.

His depth of knowledge, born of a real passion for the subject, meant that Adrian was the first preference for lawyers in other departments to consult. He could always be trusted to get the analysis right. His problem, like the nutty professor, was that the more intricate the problem, the more excitable he got in his analysis and explanation. This meant that only the brightest of the lawyers in the other departments would dare to visit him with a problem.

Such was Adrian's enthusiasm that he would not always wait to be asked for assistance. Living at the Barbican Arts Theatre complex, as he did, his home was a mere five minute stroll to the office. Being almost habitually late into the office, I would come in to find new assignments left on my seat. No sooner would I have prepared my morning cup of tea and sat down to review the papers, than Adrian would pipe up from where he was sitting with his feet on his desk, with something like:

"I think you should look at Section 776.(3)(i) (v) of the Taxes Act on that one".

After this had happened on a couple of occasions, I asked him if he could leave my work alone as I very much enjoyed testing my own ability to identify the issues. He took the admonishment in good spirit and simply went back to using his index finger to lick the remnants of his mint-chocolate morning drink from his cup.

Apart from strange drinks Adrian would also crack me up with some quaint English expressions. *"Hey-Ho"*, normally preceded an announcement of some sort, perhaps rumour of an affair within the firm. *"Ticket-i-boo"*, I came to understand to mean that everything was o.k. *"By the way I've purloined your book"* translated into *"By the way I have borrowed your book"*.

Adrian was a great companion for me. His side-kick was a petite female lawyer called Elizabeth. She would tease him no-end and he loved her even more for it because she had a razor-sharp wit. At first I thought they were an item but it emerged that she looked upon him only with sisterly admiration, even though, at our first grand office ball, they spent most of the time "dancing" together.

Every black person who has ever worked in a white establishment knows that the annual office party is an event to behold. The annual party at Lovells was an especially grand affair. The Grand Ballroom at the Hilton Park Lane, was where we would all converge: all 650 lawyers (as we then were in that first year) together with the secretaries, finance, print, post room staff et al. This was the event when the expression that white people use "letting your hair down" had real meaning although it seemed that the process always had to be aided by a liberal supply of alcohol.

This is when partners and aspiring partners with the stiffest of upper lips, and with hips to match, would suddenly assume the countenance and body movements of the possessed. The way some of them careered across the dance floor at the speed of the music merited the creation of an offence of dancing without due care and attention, assuming, that is, that you couldn't get them on a straight assault and battery charge.

The office party was the opportunity to take a closer look at the beauties that you hadn't run into in the course of the year. For me, it was always an occasion of qualified enjoyment. Though I loved to dance, I rarely did so and when I did, either with one of the lawyers that I had worked with, or more often with the black female support staff, my moves were deliberately basic. For me, it was never an occasion for me to let my hair down. The physical practicality aside, letting go, would immediately call too much attention. As the single black male lawyer, I was already far too conspicuous for my liking.

One of the great benefits of working in such a large establishment, with more than a thousand employees, was the wide variety of people one comes across; it was like being at university once more. When I started in January, 1991, there were three black female trainees, two of whom, Janice Dawkins and Tola Ogundimu, I came to know quite well. It was through them I learnt that l was the first permanent black lawyer in the firm. It didn't surprise me given my personal experience in getting into the City firms. I had also become a little bit of a celebrity in the eyes of the many black female legal secretaries and tea ladies.

It was my habit in any establishment that I happened to be in to engage with every black person that I came across. The humility that I had gained from doing security work guaranteed that however lofty the company that I found myself in at the time of any such encounter, I would always show recognition and appreciation for the support staff. Admittedly some of the female support staff commanded my recognition and appreciation for the wrong reasons. It was a function of the high salaries that these city institutions offered that some of the most stunning secretaries were to be found there – City lawyers despite their intellectual pre-occupations are only human, after all.

The high staff count meant that the firm had to have a photograph book to give everyone a chance to know who was who within each department. Without it you could have been advising a colleague over the telephone on a tax issue, and then walk past the same person later in the day without making the connection. I was told that the photographs were also useful for those, particularly the junior lawyers, in other departments looking to consult with a tax lawyer. A tax lawyer with a friendly face in the photograph book was more likely to pick up these stray consultations. Since I didn't really look like a tax lawyer, as I was often flatteringly told, I picked up quite a lot of these instructions. It was an early lesson in the importance of appearance in marketing.

The photograph book had less serious uses. Since a new edition came out with each new intake of trainee solicitors in March and September of each year, it was an opportunity for us, the established lawyers, to skip through to spot the "beauties" and the ones whose looks meant that they were obviously very bright. When I became a senior assistant, I got a direct insight into the selection process.

Law is like football in the sense that everybody can do it up to a point but, just as in football, the top earnings are only available to the very few. The annual recruitment exercise at Lovells gave me a clearer understanding of the scale of the challenge.

For the seventy-seven places available in the September, 1996, round, the firm received 2,400 applications from candidates offering the minimum requirement of an upper-second class degree and 3 A Grades at A Level. Of those 2,400 applicants, 240 received invitations for interview. The initial weeding process from the 2,400 applicants to the 240 candidates would have been done by the personnel department. The 240 applicants would then be divided between a select group of senior assistants for the first round of interviews who would make recommendations for acceptance and rejection. The second round of interviews would be conducted by a select group of partners.

The interviews would take place over the space of a couple of weeks and we would typically interview three candidates in the morning and a further three in the afternoon to allow "like" to be compared with "like". I enjoyed the interview process not least for the irony in the fact that I, who had had such difficulty in entering the fortress of the City law firms, was now a trusted gatekeeper.

The experience also brought some perspective to my own experience. The CVs were consistent in showing just how stiff the competition was and just how lucky I had been, in the circumstances, to get in at all. The usual characteristics were top prep schools, followed by first league, private and grammar schools and premier league Universities. The candidates and their parents, having made such heavy investments to get to this stage, expected a return on their investments that only the City firms could provide. With all other things being thus equal between the candidates, the chosen would be those with features that set them above the rest.

The City law firm is a major commercial enterprise whose business is the sale of the highest quality professional legal services. Like any other business it is in search for those who can help it to deliver on its product and to push its sales. Outstanding academics help to deliver a high standard product but there is no point in producing such high standard products unless you can find clients who have the means to buy them. The first amongst the equals then are those who demonstrate client-winning potential. This requires an understanding of what clients want.

Clients want a legal advisor, someone with an assured understanding of the law, who has a good understanding of their business, and who they are sufficiently comfortable with, at a relationship level, to turn to for advice. Such a person needs good technical legal skills, communication skills, presence and social skills, i.e. the complete physical and cerebral package.

Depending on the client, one or more of those skills will be more to the fore than others. For the owner-managed enterprise, the sense of comfort with the lawyer and reliable technical knowledge will be more important since he cannot afford to get it wrong.

The company secretary who is in charge of the legal affairs of a large corporation has more latitude. On the one hand his job depends on avoiding any major disasters so he will need a safe pair of hands. For this he requires technical excellence and could not give two hoots what the lawyer looks like. With the less risky instructions he has room to enjoy his position of power. For these instructions, looks and inter-personal skills are critical. These are the instructions that are available to be won by the suitor with the tighter-fitting skirt or the James Bond looks or the one who can provide the most attractive perks: a day out at Ascot or the Frankfurt Motor Show or a seat at the Wimbledon tennis finals.

Thus, in the interview, albeit without instruction from above, you were looking for those who offered these qualities of brains and presence. An excess of one quality could compensate for a deficit of the other but it is always best if you come with both in balance.

The combination that a particular recruit offers will be a major influence in determining which department he or she will end up practising in. The key bread winners in a major commercial law firm are those who make deals happen.

The company commercial lawyer is the leader of the pack through whom the advice coming from the different departments in the firm is filtered through to the in-house counsel who in turn distills the external legal input for the consumption of the Board. Having such close working relationships and affinity to the in-house counsel makes the company commercial lawyer the central cog in any corporate transaction.

A typical transaction would require input from the employment, pensions, property, intellectual property, tax and the company-commercial department. Thus the company-commercial lawyer needs to combine the skills of a project manager, team leader and client relations manager. Depending on the particular lawyer, different aspects of this portfolio of responsibilities will be called to the fore, particularly at the partner level.

While some could achieve success and yet be decent and nice to all, others built their success on being feared by their team. At the mention of their name you were supposed to be filled with foreboding and, indeed, some were. Clients ultimately wanted results and had little reason to be concerned about how those results were obtained. I was amazed to see how obnoxious colleagues could be to one another at a personal level and yet put aside their personal feelings in a convincing show of teamwork to their client. It was called being professional.

The Tax Department within a major law firm is really like a consulting clinic. Since in the developed world tax laws are extensive and tax consequences are real, every transaction whether it be a property or share based transaction or even a settlement in a litigation has to be analyzed for possible tax consequences.

The role of a good tax lawyer is to add value to a transaction by analyzing the deal and highlighting the tax issues and whenever possible, advising how the same transaction could be re-configured to achieve the same commercial outcome without triggering avoidable tax consequences.

The range of tax subjects that we were required to master was broad: Corporation Tax, Income Tax, Capital Gains Tax, VAT, Stamp Duty, Inheritance Tax, and Stamp Duty Reserve Tax. The more the government legislated or won cases to close loopholes that had been opened up by the tax lawyers, the more the tax lawyers looked to find new creative solutions to help their clients escape the Treasury's clutches or at least to mitigate the burden of the tax laws. As a result the legislation was intricate and voluminous and the related case law was extensive.

A corporate tax lawyer needed much more than the mastery of these laws. He also had to be a good general commercial lawyer in order to understand how transactions might be re-organised to achieve a different tax outcome. The experience that I had acquired at Coopers from drafting trusts, employment contracts, wills and all sorts of company resolutions therefore came in very handy.

Hitting the Ground Running

"Well you said you wanted to do corporate tax didn't you, so here's one for you".

With that Chris Major handed me the file in respect of Dynatech's proposed acquisition of a Malaysian-owned tyre manufacturing company for £1.2 million pounds on my first day.

Looking back now it was a small transaction by Lovells standards but then I had never been entrusted with so much responsibility. I knew that I would have to learn quickly and I was prepared for that. I spent the weekend digesting a book on corporate acquisitions and with the help of a few pointers from Adrian, I was able to talk knowledgeably with the client and with my colleague on the transaction from the company and commercial department.

The client was an American corporation represented by a flannel-suited middle-aged in-house law counsel with a walrus moustache. We connected very well from the outset.

In a way he was the ideal client for me to start out with. This was partly because as an American he was used to seeing black lawyers operating at this level in a way that many of his U.K. counterparts were not. It was also because he took nothing on trust. Every assertion had to be explained to his perfect understanding before he would accept it and allow you to move on; there was no room for fluff or for hiding behind the fact that this was English law which was different from U.S. law with which he was familiar.

His style suited me because I had a quick grasp of concepts and an ability to reformulate the most complicated concepts into the simplest language. On this acquisition, he was the eager and questioning student and I was the patient and confident tutor. The fact that the tutor was hurriedly teaching himself as he went along was neither here nor there.

The client was not alone in his quizzical approach. My colleague on the transaction from the company commercial department was much the same. Richard Fogl was an Australian who had joined Lovells from an Australian firm around about the same time as I started.

Coming from Australia, a country notorious for the mistreatment of its aboriginal people by its white settlers on a par with Apartheid South Africa, I had no doubt that this was his first experience of seeing a black lawyer having such a high level involvement in a commercial transaction. His surprise was all the greater given that it was the tax law aspect of the deal that I was handling. Again, because I was able to assist his understanding of the issues we got on superbly well and became great friends.

I had also attracted the curiosity of Gordon Toland, the oldest partner in Lovells tax team and one of the oldest in the firm. My arrival must have been quite revolutionary for him. He was quick to put me to the test with an assignment and when Homer nodded his approval of my analysis we got on extremely well. The tax lawyers had a habit of wandering into each other's rooms to expose any new esoteric legal argument they may be proposing to run with to friendly-fire before going public with it, and Gordon was no stranger to my room. ▩

7. EQUALLY BEFORE THE LAW

My first year at Lovells wasn't quite over when I was invited by Tola and Janice, the two black female trainees, to attend the inaugural meeting of the African, Caribbean and Asian Lawyers Group ("ACA").

My instinct was to offer my regrets because, up until this time, the public face and voice of the black members of the legal profession in England was the Society of Black Lawyers ("SBL"). It was a voice that had been out of tune with my outlook on life ever since I first encountered them at Bar School in 1985. The members of the organization being, typically, barristers in legal aid (publicly funded) practice, their vocal radicalism was in synch with their client base who needed lawyers who could speak passionately for them. Such an organization had little to offer those of us whose clients needed lawyers who spoke with less emotion.

It was the realization that the fire-spitting SBL could not properly represent the commercial lawyers within the community, or for that matter the emerging black business community, that persuaded me of the need for an organization like the ACA.

Not surprisingly the SBL leadership saw the emergence of the ACA as a "divide and rule" strategy instigated by the establishment. The fact that the ACA Lawyers Group was initiated by the Law Society's Equal Opportunities officer, a Caribbean fellow by the name of Jerry Garvey, and that its meetings were held at the Law Society's headquarters was all the proof that the SBL needed of the wicked machinations.

The situation wasn't helped by the fact that it was around about this time that the SBL were at war with the Bar Council over the Bar Finals examinations that all would-be barristers must pass before becoming eligible to be called to the Bar. They had taken the position that the exams were discriminatory in response to press reports of the higher failure rate of black students in the exams in comparison with their white counterparts.

With my own first-hand experience of the Bar exams, I was at a loss to understand how anyone could attribute their failure to pass the exams to discrimination. It was an examination of students' understanding of legal topics on which all had received the same tuition over the course of the academic year. This was nothing like the non-verbal reasoning tests that had blocked my way into the higher levels of the civil service.

The campaign had in fact been started by a group of black students who had failed the exams and the SBL had taken up their cause without, in my view, undertaking a critical review of the merits. I had to speak.

In a letter published in *The Times*, I argued that it was an insult to the many black students who took the bar exams each and every year to suggest that, having received the same tuition as their white counterparts, the exams somehow needed to be adjusted in their favour. The letter went on to say that the discrimination that there was lay not in the Bar exams but in the fact that the many black students who did pass the exams were not given equal opportunities to practise which they had demonstrated they had aptitude for.

The logic of the argument was clear but the SBL did not share it. Still I had made the point that we sometimes did more damage to the wider struggle for opportunities in Britain by not conducting basic due diligence on every voice crying wolf.

The Lessons of Babel

At the inaugural meeting of the ACA, it was nice to see black and Asian lawyers from Slaughter & May, Linklaters & Paines, Allen & Overy, Richards Butler, Eversheds, Theodore Goddard and McFarlanes as well as from local authorities, in-house legal departments and some smaller firms.

That three of us, myself, Tola and Janice, came from one firm, Lovells, was the exception which proved the rule that the black lawyer was typically one of a species in the City law firms. It confirmed the need for the network that the ACA provided. The monthly meeting was a haven where we could come off-duty as black Britons and just be ourselves. Our annual ball was where we could "let go" on the dance floor without fear of making a spectacle of ourselves.

Sometime after I had stepped down as chairman of the group my successor, Audrey Dorival, and I were invited to lunch by the managing partner of the City firm MacFarlanes. It wasn't going to be a free lunch because he had given us notice of the puzzle he , and his colleagues wanted answered. The question was why the very idea of our group for African Caribbean and Asian lawyers was not divisive and discriminatory and why it was not sufficient for ethnic minority lawyers to just be members of the Law Society like other solicitors.

As we were ushered into the partners' swish dining suite our hosts were already seated. When they stood to welcome us I noticed that one of them was wearing a Royal Air Force regimental tie. I picked up the RAF theme to break the ice and he confirmed that he met up from time to time with fellow ex-RAF to reminisce and fraternize.

When later on the exam question was brought up I asked whether he thought there was any difference between the practice of the members of the RAF club meeting separately and apart from the rest of the Armed Forces, and the ACA where those of us who shared the unique quality and experience of being minority lawyers in majority law firms met. The point was well-taken and they graciously committed to providing sponsorship for the group.

The issue that had been raised was a fair one which I know has troubled many well-meaning members of white society, who struggle to understand the complaints of members of the ethnic-minority community that they are not being allowed in, while at the same time seeming to prefer their own company. The answer is of course that a truly multi-cultural society is the abode of the gods alone and that there are limits to integration between we earthlings. It is only that we refuse to heed the wishes of the gods as relayed in the biblical story of the Tower of Babel taken from the New King James Version:

"And the Lord said, "Indeed the people are one and they all have one language, and this is what they begin to do... Come, let Us go down and there confuse their language that they may not understand

one another's speech".

Minority Lawyers in the USA

It was at the second meeting of the ACA that I had been invited to become its first chairman. I was, initially, concerned about how the position would sit with my status as a lawyer in a major City firm. The potential for embarrassment was obvious since there would be issues on which I would have to take a public stand. In the end it was my personal catalogue of hard knocks on the road to law that persuaded me to say, "Damn the consequences, we need a forum and a voice".

Leading the ACA turned out to be a fantastic challenge. We needed to grow and to do it quickly because the SBL were still hostile and suspicious. The key to growth is performance and the key to performance is good ideas and good people to implement the ideas.

Students were forever showing up at our monthly meetings to query what we were doing for them as far as getting training contracts was concerned, losing sight of the fact that we were merely volunteers doing the little we were able to do out of a sense of communal responsibility. Unfortunately many who benefited from our efforts were never seen again once they had got what they needed.

My position as chair of the ACA had been useful in persuading Lovells to send me to the American Bar Association Annual Meeting in New Orleans, USA, in 1994 to do some networking. From this conference, I got a clear grasp of just how far behind the ethnic-minority lawyers in the English legal profession were in comparison.

The first shock was to see a young black male on the speaking platform at a big session on Real Estate Investment Trusts. It occurred to me that he would have to be fairly senior for his firm to allow him to be speaking on this technical field to such an informed and important audience. Then I met a black male litigation partner in one of the largest firms in New Orleans.

As is the practice when a major lawyers' conference hits any town, the larger law firms in the locality lay on generous entertainment to induce the from-out-of-town-lawyers to visit their offices. The hope is that such hospitality will translate into referrals in the course of time. The entertainment that this law firm laid on was at the Sea

World Centre in the French Quarter in New Orleans. The sight of lawyers wining and dining with sharks swimming overhead behind reinforced glass would have made a great photo-shot for the lawyer-haters.

The partners in the practice were distinctive in their uniformly cream linen suits and starched white shirts and so it was easy to work out that he was one of the partners.

Visiting his office the following day I felt shock and awe. His room was, quite simply, a world apart in size, furnishing and comfort from the offices of the City partners in London. There was a huge executive desk which was so free of paper that you wondered what in fact it was used for. The desk was complemented by the best quality leather sofas together with an eigth-seater conference table and oak-paneled sideboards, chandeliers and crystal decanters. It was more like a penthouse than a place of work.

I was visibly taken aback by all that I was seeing and did not care to hide it. I confessed to him that this was my dream office except that there was one thing that the dream version had and his didn't, which was a high-end Hi-fi system.

"Look inside the sideboard", he said.

When I did, there it was – of the best quality that money can buy.

It was much later on in the course of my work as a tax lawyer that I got to understand why American lawyers equip their offices to such a high standard. It is because U.S. tax laws give more generous allowances for office kit and also because the U.S. lawyers spend so many more hours in their offices than their City counterparts so that the office is really a second home. The City law firms have since caught up on the long hours but without the extra personal comforts that make such long sojourns at work more tolerable.

The surprises continued because I then came across the "Minority Partners in Majority Firms Organization". This was the final straw as far as I was concerned. To meet a black partner in a major law firm of many years standing, was an experience of itself. To find that there were so many others like him as to have formed themselves into an organization, was too much for the leader of a minority lawyers' organization in the U.K., whose aim was no higher than getting a few more minority lawyers into the major law firms at the trainee level!

Beyond the significant numbers who were in practice with the major law firms, I was interested to note the many more who were "doing their own thing" either alone or in partnership. The key, it emerged, was that unlike the situation in England, once the would-be lawyer had successfully completed his law school education, he or she was at liberty to practice without having to wait for an existing practitioner to let him in by way of an offer of a pupilage or a training contract. This avoided the mismatch between law graduates and practice opportunities which so characterizes the English system. With such flexibility built into the system it is hard for the minority lawyer to lay the blame for any bottlenecks on his path to legal practice at the doors of the established law firms.

I was impressed by the equity in this arrangement. This was real equal opportunity. From the experience of my own difficulties in obtaining a training opportunity, I knew the English system was short-changing minority lawyers when compared to the American system.

Minimum Salaries

A bad situation was made worse by the impact of the Law Society's minimum salary rule under which a commitment by a firm to train a student for the mandatory two-year period came with a commitment to pay the student a salary of not less than the minimum figure set by the Law Society from time to time.

For the larger law firms the minimum salary presented no problems at all, being well below what they could afford to pay for the benefit they expected to derive from the trainees' services. In fact the largest law firms would typically pay their trainees twice the level of the minimum salary.

For the smaller law firms, this minimum salary was often well above what their businesses could carry and was often disproportionate to the earnings of the qualified fee-earners in the practice. Although the Law Society had power to grant a dispensation from the minimum salary requirement in cases of genuine hardship, most law firms preferred to dispense with the services of the trainee altogether. This they could, and did, do by simply employing the would-be trainee as a paralegal.

The ultimate loser in the arrangement was the would-be trainee who the minimum salary rule was supposed to protect from exploitation because, as a paralegal he does not get the two year commitment that the law firm gives under a training contract. More significantly, he does not get the training that would ensure that he would emerge as a fully-qualified solicitor.

Those who managed to secure such paralegal positions were in fact the luckier ones. The unfortunates are those who got nothing at all, after all their years of study, because so many small firms that might have taken them on freely negotiated terms simply withdrew from the market altogether.

The minimum salary rule was supported by two powerful groups. Some in the Law Society establishment saw it as a subtle means of containing and controlling the numbers in the profession. Then there were the existing trainees themselves, represented by the Trainee Solicitors Group, most of whom were from income groups that needed no protection.

The *raison d' être* of the Trainee Solicitors Group being the advancement and protection of the interests of those who had training contracts, they used their position on the Training Committee to defend the retention and annual increase of the minimum salary. In the best traditions of trade unions, their principal argument was that without such protection trainees would be exploited by the rapacious law firms, and already the trainees were living from hand to mouth. In the meantime, those from less privileged backgrounds like mine, who would have worked for nothing if necessary, were being denied the opportunity to train at all. We in the ACA had a special interest in getting rid of the rule because of the disproportionate number of ethnic minority law graduates who did not have training contracts and who would readily have accepted an open market wage for the opportunity to realize their ambitions.

A Troublesome Presidency

These were the arguments that were traded in the "Great Debate" on the minimum salary rule during the stormy tenure of Mr Martin Mears as President of the Law Society

Mr Mears was the senior partner of a firm in Norfolk, a place that few ethnic minorities had heard of let alone ventured into. In appearance and mannerisms he was the quintessential English solicitor, complete with the country tweed suits, pock-marked reddish face, a waistcoat with a pocket watch and chain.

He was on a mission to get to grips with the Equal Opportunities lobby that had hijacked his beloved England and its legal profession. He had announced his purpose on the route to the Presidency with a series of hard-hitting interviews on race and sex discrimination that was given a lot of press coverage. His boldest claim was that there was no such thing as discrimination in the English legal profession.

The liberals in the profession, the younger lawyers especially, were more than a touch embarrassed by Mr Mears' hard line approach and so the Trainee Solicitors Group, together with the Young Solicitors Group, organized a debate on the issue. It was to be a head-to-head confrontation at dusk between me and Martin Mears, the incoming President of the Law Society.

A key quality in any debate is to try and anticipate the line of argument of your opponent. I had prepared well by reading some of Mr Mears' utterances and articles; he failed to make the same preparation. I knew that he was going to produce statistical evidence pointing to increasing numbers of ethnic minorities in the profession and, true enough, he arrived with a briefcase full of articles, graphs and reports.

Another quality in debate is to know your audience. The audience at this debate was made up of students, trainees and young solicitors. These were the New-Labour generation who would respond more to sound-bites than to statistics and graphs.

As fate would have it, I was invited to open the case on behalf the ethnic minority lawyers. I began with an admission:

"Within the ethnic minority community in England there is racial discrimination: Blacks discriminate against Asians and vice versa. Within the Black community in England there is discrimination: Africans discriminate against West Indians and vice versa. Even within my own Nigerian community there is discrimination. Yoruba discriminate against Igbo and vice versa. The reason that discrimination exists between these communities is that difference exists and whenever there is difference it is natural for one to prefer one's own."

I continued:

"Yet Mr Mears will have us believe that across the greatest divide of all, that between people of colour and the white indigenous community, discrimination does not exist. The proposition is so incredible that it must be dismissed as soon as it is stated."

I decided to truncate the rest of my arguments so as to have Mr Mears put his case while the force of the blow was still resonating with the audience.

As he took the podium his already reddish face went much

redder. I felt a little sorry for him as he fumbled through the reams of statistics that he had brought along to prove his case. For the sound-bite audience each rustle of his papers was deafening and each statistic produced only served further to reduce the appeal of his argument. Yet he soldiered on through the allocated fifteen minutes.

An admirable quality is grace in defeat. Mr Mears showed this quality when, having stepped up to become the President of the Law Society, he appointed me to its Training Committee and invited me to chair a sub-committee to look into the abolition of the minimum salary rule. I was happy to accept his invitation.

After this debate Mr Mears was a little more discreet on issues of race and sex discrimination within the legal profession but that is not to say the issue itself went quiet.

The tradition at the Law Society was that the President's appointee as Vice President automatically became the next President. Mr Mears' Vice-President, Mr Sayers, had chosen Mrs Kamlesh Bahl, an Asian lawyer as his Vice President and had reason to believe that the storms that Martin Mears had kicked up would soon become a distant memory.

The selection of Bahl had historic portent as she was set to become the first ethnic minority President of the Law Society of England and Wales. The appointment was to make history in quite a different way as Kamlesh Bahl never made her date with destiny. Instead President and Vice President of the Law Society of England and Wales fought it out in the courts as Bahl accused Sayers of unlawful conduct in the way of race discrimination.

The Qualified Lawyer's Transfer Test

The challenge of race relations within the legal profession is a continuing one for the Law Society because in 2008, the Education and Training Policy Unit of the Solicitors Regulation Authority found themselves having to issue a consultation paper on "Requirements for lawyers qualifying as solicitors in England and Wales" because things were out of control.

As the consultation paper put it:

"There is evidence that a disproportionately high number of solicitors who qualified using the "fast track" route are the subject of professional disciplinary procedures and sanctions when compared with solicitors who have qualified using the domestic route."

The problem was not so much with lawyers, like me, who had been called to the English bar and then practiced with a U.K. firm before undertaking the Qualified Lawyers Transfer Test (QLTT) in order to formally re-qualify as a solicitor of the Supreme Court of England and Wales, and then running a law firm. It was with lawyers who had qualified as barristers/solicitors in Commonwealth countries but who without any experience of practice in England and Wales, used the QLTT short-cut to emerge as solicitors eligible to run law firms in the U.K..

The QLTT short cut to qualification was first introduced in 1990 for the old Commonwealth countries South Africa, Australia, and New Zealand. Given the shared blood and history and the regulatory standards between the profession in the mother country and the Anglo-Saxon Diaspora being broadly on par the reciprocal arrangement for qualified lawyers in one jurisdiction to have a fast track route to qualification in another jurisdiction makes sense.

Thus it was that Richard Fogl, the company-commercial lawyer on my first corporate acquisition at Lovells had been able to make the transition so smoothly from his former practice with Barker Gosling in Australia. It was in fact the insight that I gained from Richard's own journey into legal practice in England that was the origin of the crisis with the QLTT.

It was at a Law Society Training Committee meeting, when we were discussing the interminable problem of the shortage of Training Contracts and the special problems that African Caribbean and Asian lawyers were encountering, that I queried how it was that in the limited time that I had been practicing in the City I had encountered lawyers from Australia and South Africa but never from Nigeria or India.

"Oh, we must look at the QLTT Regulations because there is no reason why they should not apply to these countries", was the response.

I was happy that the door was to be opened a little wider for our members. The legal education and training providers, who were well represented on the Committee, were happy too because they could see the fees to be made from selling the QLTT route in the new markets that were about to be opened up. For its part, the Law Society was happy to be seen to be making opportunities more equal.

What the Society failed to see was that the regulatory standards in the new Commonwealth countries were nowhere near those that it enforced. The Law Society also had little sense of the huge take up that was in prospect for the QLTT route from the new Commonwealth; A Level of take up that owed much to the economic boom in Britain even as prospects were fading in most of these countries.

It was only after I started running my own law firm that I myself came to appreciate just how demanding the accounting and other regularity burdens are on a U.K. solicitor. A law firm holding and managing client money from large numbers of clients at the same time has challenges not dissimilar from a bank.

Having come from a mega City law firm background, where I had had nothing to do with accounting entries or client money, straight into my own firm where I was expected to hit the ground running on such matters, I could empathise with the lawyers from the new Commonwealth countries, to whom the strict Law Society rules on dealings with "client money" would have seemed like much-ado-about-nothing.

I have no doubt that the high incidence of disciplinary actions against those from the new Commonwealth who came through the QLTT route had less to do with dishonesty than with want of experience. I was only fortunate that the Law Society's inspection of our compliance record in this regard came close to our 10th anniversary as a firm by which time we had got a better handle on things.

The Equal Opportunities Challenge

The Law Society were not alone in their desire to bridge the racial divide within the profession.

We in the African, Caribbean and Asian Lawyers' Group were also trying to build relationships with the other ethnic minority lawyers groups; the Society of Asian Lawyers, and the Society of Black Lawyers, now under the leadership of an Asian Lawyer Makbool Javaid. What Makbool gained in being less combative than his predecessor, Peter Herbert, he lost in being much more verbose.

One of the initiatives that I brought to the ACA table was a C.V referral scheme based on an idea that I had seen in operation at the American Bar Association Annual Meeting in New Orleans, USA. We had decided to offer participation in the scheme to the other ethnic minority lawyer groups as a means of drawing the other groups closer.

The scheme recognised that between those looking for training contracts and the firms who would hire them it was a buyer's market. As such the City law firms really had no need to cast their net any wider than they had been doing since they had always found more than enough fish to meet their needs from the thousands of applications that each of these firms received for a handful of openings.

The problem for students from the ethnic minority community was that only very few of them went to the universities that were the traditional waters of the City law firms who recruited the greatest number of trainees. From the viewpoint of the law firms, there was no business case to justify the extra resources that could be required to trawl through the newer universities where most ethnic minority students studied. If the gap was to be bridged it was Mohammed who would have to move to the mountain.

The CV referral scheme invited ethnic minority students, who possessed the minimum upper-second class honours degree that the City law firms required, to send their CVs to the group with an open covering letter. The CVs and covering letters were collated in a ring-binder folder each year and a copy of the folder was sent to the Training Partner in each participating firm for consideration without obligation.

If the CV of any student was sufficiently attractive the firm would take the application forward as it saw fit. In this way the firms had nothing to lose from the scheme but something to gain in terms of the assistance we were giving in finding lawyers of potential. The ethnic minority lawyers groups had a lot to gain because we were delivering a tangible resource to our members. It was a win-win opportunity.

This is how we presented the scheme at the meeting at Clifford Chance's main conference room between the representatives of the three ethnic minority lawyers groups and the training partners of the top twenty-five City law firms which the Law Society's Training Committee had facilitated.

What a meeting it was. The room was the size of a typical secondary school's main assembly hall with an ornate oval shaped conference table that spanned the length of the room befitting the firm's status as the largest law firm in the world. It sat fifty comfortably with room to spare. The audio facilities were such that, when the meeting was called to order by Michael Mathews, a member of the Law Society's

Council and Clifford Chance's then senior partner, we could almost hear each other breathing.

In a meeting of this scale, the chairman will always have his work cut out to give all who wish to speak an opportunity to do so not least because there will be some who will always take ten minutes to say what others could say in one. Makbool was in full flow on another oration lecturing the City firms on their failure to do enough, when his mobile phone went off suitably amplified by the microphones. That Makbool joined with the chorus of laughter at this inspired truncation of his sermon showed his sense of humour. It no doubt contributed to his status as an employment law partner now with one of the city firms that were present at that meeting.

Equal opportunities remains little more than an aspiration which lies beyond the reach of the societies that have declared commitments to it. These are the societies where people of visibly different racial origins have sought to drink from the same goblet of opportunity in defiance of the laws of the Tower of Babel.

The Black-Led Commercial Law Firm

Even though the gods have given warning that this model of society is for them alone, the equal opportunities industry in Britain, as in most multi-racial societies, continues to grow to keep the dream alive. The fact is that business and government departments find it much easier to sub-contract the challenge to intermediaries than to face the challenge head on. In my time in practice I had obtained a fairly good insight into the comparative performance of black lawyers and law firms in different territories. It had, for example, been a source of puzzlement to me why, despite the presence of a very well-to-do black community in the U.S., the black law firms had not kept pace with the financial growth of the African-American community.

Yes, there were very successful litigators like Johnny Cochrane of O.J. Simpson fame, but where were the commercial law firms that one would have expected to have emerged as the community came into money? Who were the lawyers representing the LL Cool Js, the Mary J Bliges, the Eddie Murphys and the Whitney Houstons, Cuba Gooding Jr.s and the Will Smiths in their multi-million dollar commercial dealings?

Reginald Lewis, a Harvard law graduate with his New York law

On my call to the Nigerian Bar in 1986. From left to right:
Mrs Ijose, me, my mother, Dr Ijose

firm, was the exception that proved the rule until his tragic and premature death at the age of fifty on 19 January, 1993. And this was in spite of the affirmative action policies that had been designed to compensate for the fact that the black community had been held back from the starting line until the 1960s.

The position, I was to discover, was no different in South Africa. Nelson Mandela had been released from Robben Island; the Apartheid regime had been consigned to the archives and expectations were high for the black South African lawyers. They were, after all, in their own country where they were the majority people.

My first insight into the South African legal profession came in 2003 at the International Bar Association Conference in Durban. The largest law firms, like Edward Nathan, would not have looked out of place in England or America. These firms were as old as the colony itself and they were no less dominant. Webber Wentzel, one of the largest commercial law firms in South Africa, had been established as far back as 1868. With such old and very mighty oaks around, there was precious little room for new black saplings to emerge and, with the economy still firmly in the hands of the white minority community, it was going to take extra-ordinary ability and a fair political wind for the black lawyers to break through.

A promising wind had started to blow in 2003 when the Black Economic Empowerment Act was passed by the now ANC-controlled South African Government. This was affirmative action but with the difference that the object was to redress the economic balance in the multi-racial country in favour of the majority ethnic group rather the minority. The expectations were great and the black South African lawyers had prepared themselves for the new opportunities as best they could.

I met one of them while on a trade mission to Johannesburg. Kashane Manamela was a top grade lawyer with great insight. He had gone right into the lion's den, the Afrikaans-speaking University of Pretoria and had emerged with an excellent law degree. He had positioned himself as a corporate lawyer and had qualified as an insolvency practitioner to boot. Having trained and worked for some years with a highly-regarded mainstream law firm, he felt ready to step out to lead from the front and build the dream of a top-grade black-led commercial law firm in his homeland. It was, alas, to remain a dream.

Manamela & Co started off all right. The brochures and website looked right and they were well-positioned in the city district of the capital Tswane (the old Pretoria). He had also been making the right strategic moves. He had made the practice multi-racial with a white and an Asian partner and he had got himself into the loop with the embassies of South Africa's main trading partners which was how he came to be invited to the reception for the British Trade Mission that I attended.

However, after nearly ten years of his best efforts and a staff complement of thirteen, he was finding that he was simply making a living along Hard Street. The much anticipated take-off that would have moved the firm onto Easy Street continued to be elusive.

Far from realizing his dream of competing for the best lawyers with the established law firms he found that he was struggling to hold onto his partners and partner-grade lawyers in the face of the opportunities that the established law firms were offering.

These firms had known precisely what they needed to do to turn the threat that the Black Economic Empowerment programme posed into advantage. They simply opened up to bring on board the best black lawyers, particularly those with strong links to the upper echelons of the ANC. In one remarkable case one of the oldest law firms set aside forty percent of the equity in the practice for the black lawyers. The result was that the work flowed to these law firms like never before; so much so that it was the established firms who, at the end of the day had reason to give the thumbsup to the Black Economic Empowerment programme.

It was now harder than ever for those like Manamela who valued their independence to get a look in. It was not long before my friend wrote to me to say that it was looking as if he would have to throw the towel in and accept one of the many offers he had been receiving from the white law firms.

Having noted the same challenges amongst law firms in Kenya and the Caribbean, I was led to the conclusion that if proper analysis were made of black commercial law firms and lawyers across the world, it will be those in Nigeria and other parts of West Africa that would emerge as the most significant players. They owe this not to any equal opportunities claims or programmes but simply to the squadron of mosquitoes with their malaria missiles that have allowed them to be the dominant players in their own land. ▨

8. A BRIEF ENCOUNTER WITH THE LAW LORDS AND MANDELA'S LAWYER

'An Englishman's home is his castle' is an old saying because it is true only of the England of old. Then the Englishman loved his home, whether large or small and whether he owned it or simply rented it.

Things changed with the economic revolution that Prime Minster Margaret Thatcher ushered in the 1980s. From then on the Englishman's home became his shrine where he worships the goddess of unearned wealth. Now he loves his home because of its tradeable value.

It is the use of a home as a gambling chip that explains why the Englishman is much more likely than his continental counterparts to own his home or, at least, to aspire to own it. The bricks and mortar is the repository of his devotion and, ever since the property boom of the early 1980s, it has been the principal element in his wealth.

The frenzy for home ownership having been kicked off by government tax incentives in the form of exemption from capital gains tax on homes and tax relief for interest payments on borrowings to purchase the home, it became an article of faith that property in England is the one thing that always goes up and never goes down.

To keep this sacred cow of England in robust health has become every government's duty. The political equation is simple: If house prices go up your votes go up. If house prices go down your votes go down and your party is thrown out. To stay in power each administration has to find a creative way to keep the feel-good over the value of homes going.

All was well with John Major's administration which followed Margaret Thatcher's until it decided that Britain should, after all, join the European single currency project that gave birth to the Euro. To explain what happened you have to come with me to a playground in Europe.

The children's roundabout is the most exhilarating ride in the playground. When the ride is in its standing position, the smaller kids climb on board in excited expectation. Three of the biggest kids may then set the ride in motion by pushing the side handlebars in a common direction.

Slowly the ride gathers momentum and when it has reached a desirable speed, the three consider their work done and jump onto the sideboards to enjoy the ride. This is when the last kid, who had been on the swings all along while the rest had been getting the roundabout going, decides that now that things are looking good, he would quite like to join this particular ride after all.

The other kids are not going to stop or slow the ride for him. To make matters worse some local "hoodies" have come along to make the ride go even faster to the excitement of those already on board whilst making it more risky for the last kid to jump on board. The hope of the hoodies is that he will go ahead and jump on, because they are hoping that he will mis-time his jump and be flung off the ride. It in fact went beyond a hope because they had taken bets on this outcome.

The boy on the swing thought he had got a good measure of the speed of the roundabout and that he had timed his run up perfectly, but he was wrong. Having jumped in, his desperate attempts to cling on failed and he was flung off by the momentum of the ride ,cracking his head on the concrete floor in the process. The hoodies laughed as he was carried away in an ambulance.

This imaginary scenario in an imaginary playground somewhere in Europe illustrates what happened in the real adult world of high finance when Britain attempted to join the Euro club.

The smaller European countries had climbed on board right from the onset of the project. France, Germany and Italy had together done the hard work in getting the Euro moving whilst Britain had been sitting on the swings. To join the Euro, now that it was on the move, it was critical that the British pound sterling entered at the right exchange rate to the euro.

The Chancellor, Norman Lamont had decided on the rate at which to jump. The hoodies, the currency speculators, like George Soros and his mates, were spinning the wheel ever-faster by dumping the pound in the conviction that the Chancellor had got the entry rate wrong and Britain would not be able to hold on. Lamont tried to call their bluff by increasing interest rates to persuade speculators to hold onto the pound. In quick time interest rates that were barely comfortable at 7 percent were hiked up to 15 percent and many who had been sucked into the property-owning dream started to fall into arrears and some began to fall, very deliberately, off buildings. As banks began to repossess the homes, house prices began to fall. In the meantime another problem had developed.

An unintended, though foreseeable, consequence of homes not simply being places to live in but as investment assets also is that "the English dream" becomes unaffordable to many. Those who are most affected by this side-effect are those who have least control over their earnings i.e. the lower-waged. Their dilemma was made even worse by the fact that the same government was at the same time holding down their wage demands in an effort to tame the inflationary flames that had sprung up from the property boom.

With the investor-landlords fixing their rent by reference to their mortgage commitments rather than to meet the country's housing needs, a situation had been created where a critical segment of the population could neither afford to buy nor rent a decent home.

When foresight fails hindsight simply has to do the best it can. The government's answer was a new tax incentive to encourage the provision of affordable homes for the rental market in the form the Business Expansion Scheme (BES).

Rescuing the Banks

The BES tax incentive was originally configured as a means of attracting private investment into the more risky businesses. These were the enterprises to which the banks were typically reluctant to commit their money. Government calculated, rightly, that with the right tax incentives in place, ordinary folk could be induced to commit their money into those very places that the banks feared to tread.

The incentive came in the form of a pledge of exemption from capital gains tax on any gain made on BES shares if the investment was successful. There was the added assurance that if the investment failed the investor would be given tax relief for loss on the shares against his taxable income. All this, combined with the promise that the punter could get up to a 40 percent tax subsidy in the meantime on the amount he subscribed for the shares, made the inducement irresistible.

Conscious that professional advisers would find ways to stretch these concessions and incentives beyond the limits that it intended, the government took care to ensure that the BES legislation contained very detailed rules to regulate the types of enterprises and investors that could participate in the scheme. The last thing that it originally intended was to provide generous tax concessions for investments that were less risky because they were backed by safe assets. This caution was abandoned when the BES scheme was opened up to companies providing homes to be let on what were known as Assured Shorthold Tenancies.

The government saw the move as a way of killing two birds with one stone. The glut of properties that had been repossessed by the banks, and which was dragging down house prices, would be repackaged by the banks into new BES companies. The BES companies would set themselves up as corporate landlords letting out these properties until the property market could resume its upwards-always journey.

So, in short, the government would give the public the tax breaks on the BES shares to encourage them to invest in these companies, so that these companies would use the sums raised to buy the repossessed properties from the banks to be let out on Assured Shorthold Tenancies.

The banks had every reason to work with the government on a solution since they were not exactly in the business of owning lots of residential properties. It didn't take long before the smart banking executives came up with a trick to make the shares even more appealing to the punters.

Although the BES Scheme legislation said that a taxpayer would only get tax relief if he held the shares for five years, the banks provided investors with the means to sidestep this condition. They would lend the punter an amount of money equal to whatever he had paid for the shares. The loan would be recovered by the bank solely from the sale proceeds of the shares after the expiry of the five year mandatory holding period. In the meantime the banks would hold the shares as security. To put it more simply, the banks were agreeing to stand in the queue for the mandatory five year period in place of the punters, for a cut of course!

Suddenly, a tax incentive that had been tailored to encourage investment in riskier enterprises had been converted into a money-for-nothing, safe, tax-subsidized, money-in-and-money-out scheme on which the banks and the professional advisers were getting fat. Barclays and Nat West were the main players in the banking circles and we at Lovells were the main players within the legal circuit. The feast had been going on for some time and the thinking was that it would go on for some time to come.

Embarrassed into action, the Chancellor suddenly announced in his budget speech that tax relief would no longer be available for shares issued "on or after 16 March, 1993," under these loan-backed schemes.

A new section 299A of the Taxes Act was pushed out in the following terms:

"An individual shall not be entitled to relief in respect of any shares in a company issued on or after 16 March 1993 if –

> *(a) There is a loan made by any person, at any time in the relevant period, to that individual or to any associate of his; and*
>
> *(b) The loan is one which would not have been made on the same terms, if that individual had not subscribed for those shares or had not been proposing to do so."*

The race was now on to push the last few schemes that were in the pipeline through the closing gates.

The Homeshare Ltd BES Schemes, sponsored by Barclays and Nat West, were to be the last rush. Everything had been lined up to get the schemes through the gate before Big Ben sounded its first gong of the midnight bell on 15 March 1993.

The offer to the public had gone out and the investing public had answered the call of this last train to tax-subsidized heaven. They had applied for their desired number of shares and had sent in their cheques for the subscription monies; the cheques had been cashed and they had received their letters of allotment from the company confirming the number of shares that had been set aside for them.

Big Ben had struck its twelfth gong to announce the end of 15 March, 1993, and the beginning of 16 March, when hell broke loose. The Ides of March have always been tumultuous times in British folklore.

The registrars of the principal company had omitted to enter the name of the nominee company on to the register of members before the midnight mark on 15 March. Had they done it at any time before midnight all would have been well. Had they done it after the midnight gong before they "fessed" up to the lawyers that they hadn't done it, no one would have known. Now it was too late because the Inland Revenue required a certificate from the law firm advising on the scheme to confirm that all the statutory requirements had been met for the tax relief.

The big question now was, had these shares been issued in time to qualify for the tax relief? Put another way, the question was, at what point does a share become issued according to the laws of England?

The Issue of Shares

Considering the antiquity of the "company limited by shares" concept under English law, a concept that had, through the agency of the British Empire, become recognized throughout the business world, the expectation was that there would be a clear and established answer to what would seem an elementary question. In fact there wasn't. It was as well that there wasn't as it was to prove my chance to strut my stuff for my true calling as a legal problem-solver.

The Inland Revenue were in no mood to grant any concessions. As far as they were concerned the gate had closed and the shares had not been issued on time. We, on our side, acting for the banks, and ultimately for the punters, insisted that the shares had been issued.

Our first approach was to try and persuade the Revenue to see things our way. It started with a meeting with their top minds at Somerset House, the Inland Revenue's HQ on the Embankment of the River Thames. As we exchanged arguments on the matter with Mr Adrian West and his team I couldn't help reflecting on how I had struggled with the psychometric tests that had blocked my attempt to gain employment at the Revenue's Inspector grade.

We followed the meeting up with a letter setting out our detailed arguments based on the Legal Opinion provided by Robin Potts QC of Erskine Chambers, one of the top barristers in the field of English Company Law. His argument was as follows:

"The issue of Certificates is not *necessary for shares to be "issued", shares will* "normally" *i.e. but not* exclusively *be treated as issued*

when registration is effected. It is plain that, dependent on the given context, actual registration is not to be equated with "issue".

He concluded that:

"The fact that the allottees or issuees had not actually been registered is irrelevant. In other words, "issue", in this context, occurs where an applicant becomes unconditionally obliged as distinct from merely entitled to submit to registration as a holder of securities".

The Revenue were not persuaded and so there was no alternative but for the two sides to fight it out at the High Court.

Neil Fagan was the partner in charge of the litigation team. He was confident that he had the best man for the job in Robin Potts QC and, true enough, Potts did the business as the High Court ruled that the shares were issued before 16 March, 1993. In a judgment handed down on 30 July, 1993, Mr Justice Rattee decided that the shares were issued at:

"The point of time at which a mutual obligation between the applicant and the company arises obliging the applicant to take the shares concerned and the company to cause them to be registered in his name or that of his nominee".

It was '1-0 to the Arsenal' but the Inland Revenue were not about to throw in the towel. They appealed to the Court of Appeal.

Having delivered the goods the first time around, there was no question of anyone other than Potts QC arguing our corner. To our shock and amazement, and to the Inland Revenue's delight, the Court of Appeal ruled by a majority of 2 to 1 that the shares had not been issued before 16 March, 1993, as reported in [1994] Simon's Tax Cases 184. Lord Justice Dillon delivered the main judgment in favour of the Inland Revenue. As far as he was concerned the loan-back facility that the banks had introduced was nothing short of a tax avoidance scheme. In his words:

"financiers and their advisers soon developed schemes which, by exit arrangements, would have the effect that financiers would invest to obtain relief from income tax....without running any risk of losing their investments if the qualifying companies in whose shares they had nominally invested failed to prosper or expand".

Now it was 1:1 as between the people and the Inland Revenue or 2:2 on aggregate if you were to take account of the individual judgments that has been pronounced on this issue.

The match had to go to extra time before the Law Lords at the House of Lords.

The hierarchy of the English civil justice system starts with the deputy district judge in the County Court trying small civil disputes, through to the district judge, the assistant recorder, the recorder, the circuit judge, the High Court judge and the judge of the Court of Appeal. At the pinnacle of the judicial tree sit the Law Lords. These are the ultimate custodians of the laws of England. Parliament may speak through its legislature but it is the Law Lords who ultimately give meaning to what Parliament says. Appeals from their decisions lie to God alone (except on a matter of European law in which case you go to Brussels).

The Best Pound-for-Pound Lawyer

This case was too important for any expense to be spared and, with Barclays Bank and Nat West Bank as the clients, money was no object. A special meeting of the key directors and legal advisors on the banks' side, and the key partners at Lovells was convened. At that meeting the "Generals" decided that we had to add more fire power to the team of barristers we already had: we needed the best of the best and, by common acclaim, that man was Sir Sydney Kentridge QC.

The first that I knew of the development was when Peter Fisher, the tax partner with responsibility for the BES Schemes, told me that Mr Kentridge needed a briefing note explaining how the BES Schemes worked. As I was the solicitor principally concerned with the BES Scheme law, the task of explaining the rationale, origins and workings of BES Schemes for the "first advocate of all advocates" fell to me.

I had never met him but, based on what I had read of him, he was my hero and model lawyer: a big lawyer with a big conscience. I first came across him in the autobiography of Nelson Mandela, *Long Walk to Freedom,* where he had blown away my youthful generalizations about race.

At the height of the international campaign against the Apartheid regime (once I had got my political education up to speed) I had come to regard the white South African as the vilest creature to have stalked the earth. Africa was the land of the Africans, pure blacks like me, and yet here were these Europeans who had ventured across from their homeland to dehumanize the owners of the land to satisfy their greed. As one who had spent his formative years in the village in Nigeria, I knew only too well how the dispossessed of Southern Africa would have felt through the loss of their family lands. Since all land belonged to one community or other and it was held to be farmed and not to be traded, the disposssesed cannot readily find land elsewhere.

Yet in Mandela's book I found myself reading about how this most brilliant and highly successful white South African lawyer had put monetary considerations aside to defend Mandela at his trial by the evil Apartheid government on a trumped-up charge of treason. It swelled my heart hugely to learn of this man's dogged determination to defend the purity of justice by standing beside this representative of the most oppressed of peoples, come what may.

This wasn't to be Mr Kentridge's only stand on the side of justice and humanity. He had also been counsel for the local community at the enquiry into the Sharpeville massacre and at the inquest into the death of Steve Biko after a cowardly beating in custody by the then South Africa police force.

In fact Sydney Kentridge consistently took time out from the lucrative commercial instructions that were forever calling for his service to take pro bono cases for the victims of state and colonial oppression. The last that I read of him he was acting for the Chagos Islanders in the case that they had brought against the British Government. They were demanding the right to return to their native island from which they had been forcibly ejected to make way for a base for the U.S. Navy. This was the kind of injustice that Sir Sydney Kentridge would simply never walk away from.

By lending himself to such just causes this great lawyer helped to restore moral content to the study and practice of the law for me.

What marked him out as the ultimate lawyer was that when it came to matters of hard commerce he had few rivals. In the run up to our case before the Law Lords, *Legal Business Magazine*, the gospel of City lawyers, had proclaimed him as "Pound-for-pound, the best lawyer in the United Kingdom". This was the lawyer that I had to prepare the briefing paper for on the law and practice relating to BES Schemes.

As I sat down to prepare the briefing note, I could not but marvel at Sir Sidney Kentridge's ability to move effortlessly across legal practice areas: from treason trials to international human rights, to high-end company and tax law. In an age where lawyers were becoming more and more anal in their mastery of increasingly narrow aspects of the law, here was a ring marshall that was ready to take on any opponent at any time. Here he was now taking over a case, midstream, from an acknowledged leading expert in company law with no prior knowledge of the underlying BES Scheme law and practice.

Having such a close involvement in the whole matter of the BES Schemes, I had read all the judgments up to Court of Appeal level. Just as I used to do when a law student, I critically reviewed each of the judgments and I formed the view that the majority decision of the Court of Appeal was wrong. As I prepared the briefing note for Sir Sydney, I found myself going beyond my brief. I started to develop my own arguments to show why the decision was wrong.

My dyslexia-assisted reasoning helped me to see the answer from a straight-forward reading of the key sections of the Act concerning the register of members and, in particular, from the data that was required to be entered into the register.

I noted that what was required to be recorded was *"the name of the member"*, *"the number of shares in respect of which he is a member"* and *"the date on which he became a member"*.

It struck me that these provisions were premised upon the fact that the person in respect of whom these details were to be recorded had logically to have become a member of the company, i.e. a shareholder, before the point at which these particulars were actually recorded. In other words, it was not the act of recording the prescribed particulars that made the subscriber of shares a "member" and neither was it the point at which the shares were physically issued to him that made him a shareholder.

I set out my reasoning in the briefing note and added the following observations:

> *The language of section 352 presupposes the existence of a member at the time when his details are required to be entered in the register.*
>
> *If for reasons of fraud or gross negligence a company fails to keep a Register of Members as required but "issues" shares to "shareholders", does the judgment mean that the company has no issued share capital, shareholders or members until such time as the register is made up?*
>
> *Why should the Register of Members have greater significance*

for a company with a share capital vis-a-vis a company without a share capital?

A day or two later I heard that Sydney Kentridge had said that these arguments were precisely what he needed. Now the whole team of lawyers was directed to trawl through the laws of England to find material to develop my line of attack on the Court of Appeal's reasoning.

I felt a quiet satisfaction because I had never been in any doubt that when it comes to technical legal issues and arguments I was up there with the best. If proof were required that advanced reasoning can be found amongst those coming from the poor villages of the world and through inner-city comprehensives just as it can be found amongst those who have attended the best English prep and public schools, here it was.

Lovells had a tradition of giving honour to whomever honour was due. Much honour was given to me at the time and much more honour was to follow. First was the opportunity to meet Mr Kentridge.

It was Peter Fisher and I who went to meet Sir Sydney Kentridge at his chambers to discuss the intricacies of the BES Schemes and legislation in more detail. This time my name served me well as Mr Kentridge was in no doubt as to the identity of the author of his briefing paper. I took his extended hand as he gave me a special welcome. He spoke with gravitas and yet listened to every contribution with patience. The encounter convinced me that the truly wise are great listeners.

As I sat with him in his chambers I began to wonder about the great issues of English law that he had had cause to consider in this splendid isolation. I called to mind my days in the law library at the London Metropolitan University when I had seen myself being instructed to argue these great issues of English law. I wondered how my career would have evolved had I had the opportunity of being tutored by this master advocate.

Throughout my law studies I had been in no doubt that I had it within me to become one of the great advocates. The x-ray vision, which was the compensating flip side of the dyslexic mind, was the basis of this conviction. Yet here I was on the other side of the profession and only through a stroke of fortune getting a chance to show what I could do.

I reflected on how transient the levelling quality of education was because, while education does bring people from diverse social backgrounds together in a common degree programme or course of professional study, the reality, in an old country like England, is that the roads of life soon enough part again. Those who had come onto the junction on the high road almost invariably continue their journey on the high road. Those who came via the low road typically return to the low road of career opportunities but now with the added burden of knowing how the others live.

I returned from my excursions of the mind, to the reality of my position as senior assistant City tax lawyer who always wanted to be an advocate. Then and there I resolved to resume my journey to the English Bar.

City tax law was something I had got into as a default career option because the English Bar had not let me in. It was something I could do but it was not something that came as naturally as seeing arguments. This case convinced me that I was playing out of position: I was an attacking midfielder playing in the position of a central defender. The difficulties that I had had in gaining entry into the legal profession had convinced me that I would ultimately have to run my own firm to find true fulfillment in the law. Much, however, remained to be done by way of preparation.

Before the Law Lords
The second honour came shortly before the day of the hearing before the Law Lords.

"I think you should go and hear your arguments being presented to the Law Lords", Peter Fisher said almost casually.

Peter had never been the most excitable of the Lovells partners. With his permanently bored expression, the conversations that I had with him were always a little laboured. On the occasions when I joined the team for a Friday night drink in the Bottlescrew wine bar, my instinct had been to stay as far away from him as possible. Yet he was a nice fellow. He must also have been charming in his own way because he scored with a bubbly trainee that we had. Tracy Johnston was as blonde and pretty as Peter was dour and grey. Their relationship was testimony to the pulling power of opposites. Since I knew her to be a very good tax lawyer with a very sharp legal brain, it was clearly more than a power relationship. I heard through the grapevine that they have become a permanent item.

I savoured the day of the hearing before the Law Lords. Had

my career followed the path that I had expected and worked for, a day before the Law Lords would have been just another day at work. The career having taken a different turn, it was a day that came with much expectation. I donned my best suit that morning. As I left the house in my pin-striped suit with my "walking-stick umbrella", as my father used to call it, I still felt as if I was the one who was billed to present the argument.

The House of Lords, in its judicial function, is one of those quirks of the English constitutional arrangement. Though the separation of powers between the Legislature, the Executive and the Judiciary is one of the cornerstones of the English system, yet the members of the House of Lords are drawn from each of the three sectors and its functions are overlapping. The theory is only reconciled with the practice by the fact that in the performance of its judicial function the House is made up of only the most senior judges in the land even though the physical sitting takes place within the Parliament building itself.

The other oddity about the House of Lords in its capacity as the highest court in the land is that neither in the physical layout nor in the attire of the judges does it look anything like a court. For a country whose etiquette and class code is famous for its pomposity, complete with silk stockings and shoulder length wigs et al, the apex court is completely anti-climactic.

At one end of the large oak-paneled Committee room in the Parliament building which was the court room, five wooden cubicles were arranged in a Stonehenge-like arc. Ten yards from the centre of the semi-circle was a wider-than-normal solitary wooden lectern from which the best advocates in the land took it in turns to address the Law Lords on the most important cases. A few yards back from this lectern on either side were the church-like benches on which the supporting cast of junior counsel, solicitors, clients and interested members of the public silently cheered and booed each cerebral blow.

At the signal from the usher, we all rose as Their Lordships filed in, un-robed and un-wigged. The ones like Lord Woolf who had been in the papers were instantly recognizable. The others were not except to those who were regular visitors.

Each went to his cubicle where his papers had been arranged meticulously. As Sir Sidney Kentridge rose to take the lectern and began his address I had a sense of the reverence that the Law Lords had for him. This was obviously someone whom they regarded as one of their peers, if not their superior, and this was clearly just another of the many conversations that they had been having over the years on what the law of England should be.

I couldn't help wondering what their demeanour would have been had I, Akindele Ogunetimoju, been the one who was before them at the lectern presenting the argument instead of Sir Sydney Kentridge.

Experience teaches that the way in which any argument is received is influenced greatly by the regard in which the person to whom the argument is being addressed holds the person presenting the argument. Whether or not Jesus Christ was indeed the Son of God, he was clearly a person of awesome standing to have made the case as persuasively as he did or else he would have been regarded by many more as a madman. In fairness to Christ, it was not he that made the claim but those who came after him.

You can read about great advocates and you can read their arguments in the law reports and from these secondary sources get an idea of their greatness. This is how I came to know the much that I know about the greatness of Lord Wilberforce and Lord Denning the two judges whose reasoning I most admired amongst English judges. However, nothing can equal seeing and hearing one of the greats on his feet especially since oratory is a key ingredient of advocacy.

It is the moment of theatre when the advocate is speaking and all else in the room have submitted their hearing and attention to what he has to say. His thoughts, his words, and the way he utters them, are the object of such close scrutiny by all present looking for a flaw or blemish in his linguistic artistry.

As Sir Sydney Kentridge's voice filled the room in measured delivery, my imagination strayed in and out of Mandela's treason trial. I imagined how the same formidable legal mind would have presented the best arguments in the same majestic fashion.

It is, however, a handicap of law that it is ultimately no more than the handmaiden of politics. Just as the best arguments delivered by the best advocate could not save Mandela from a guilty verdict and life sentence on Robben Island, so it was to be that my arguments as delivered by the same advocate did not win the day before the Law Lords. This was reported in [1994] 3 *All England Reports 1*.

Lord Templeman, who had the reputation of being pro-Revenue, delivered the first judgment:

"In the present case it was argued on behalf of the bank that once an applicant has paid in full and shares have been allotted to him he was 'complete master of the shares'. But no one was a master of the shares until registration; until then the applicant was only entitled under a contract of which specific performance could be granted, to procure the nominee to be entered upon the register whereupon and not sooner the nominee would become 'master of the shares' acting on behalf of the applicant."

Lord Jauncey came next. He declared:

"My Lords, I have gone rather laboriously through these cases because it seems to me that there is in them nothing to support the view that a share can never be issued until the allottee's name had been registered".

Then came Lord Slynn of Hadley. Given the importance of the case, the thirteen-line Judgment he delivered was a little surprising. In essence he said:

"My Lords, I have had the advantage of reading in draft the speeches of my noble and learned friends Lord Templeman and Lord Jauncey of Tullichettle. Despite the forceful opinion of Lord Jauncey, I agree with Lord Templeman that for the reasons he gives these appeals should be dismissed."

Lord Woolf as befitted his reputation as the author of England's Civil Procedure Rules, provided more jurisprudence in a detailed judgment. He said:

"My Lords, I have had the advantage of reading in draft the speeches of my noble and learned friends Lord Templeman and Lord Jauncey of Tullichettle. They review the relevant authorities and clearly identify the reasons why it is possible to reach different views as to what should be the outcome of these appeals. I agree with the analysis which they contain of the previous authorities. I also agree with the reasons given by Lord Jauncey for allowing these appeals."

The last of the judgments was a long time coming because the Law Lord was away on his summer holidays. It was on this judgment that the case was to turn. Although the Judgments were supposed to be top secret until they were formally handed down, somehow we had managed to get word that the score was 2:2, i.e. 4:4 on aggregate taking account of the judgments in the High Court and the Court of Appeal, and that we were simply waiting on the Judgment of Lord Lloyd of Berwick.

When it came the judgment, though a little longer than Lord Slynn's, still fell well short of expectations given that it was to be the decider. He said:

"My Lords, in a case in which four judges have taken one view of the meaning of a single word, and an equal number of judges have taken another view, it would be presumptuous to say that I have found the solution easy. Nevertheless, I have no doubt that, for the reasons given by Dillon LJ in the Court of Appeal, the question must be answered in favour of the Crown."

So there it was, the issue had finally been decided 5:4 in the Revenue's favour. We were disappointed and none more so than me. Though we had lost 3:2 in the House of Lords and 5:4 an aggregate, my contribution was still being toasted within Lovells.

Further honour came in the form of an invitation from Dan Mace, the most highly regarded of the partners in the corporate team, for me to give a talk to all the corporate lawyers in the firm on the case of Barclays Bank Plc and Nat West Bank Plc v Inland Revenue Commissioners.

Back on the Road Again

By this stage, talk had begun of my becoming the first black partner at Lovells, and bets were being taken. My biggest supporter was Catherine Allinson, a partner in the Banking practice.

The talk was ironic for me in a number of ways. First I was still harbouring the secret of the strategy that Stephen Rodney and I had adopted to get me through the barriers into City law in the first instance. That experience had led me to resolve that I would only be passing through the City on a journey to a place where I would have better control of my fortune. Besides, Graham Huntley, a partner in the litigation practice had, technically speaking, already achieved the feat of being the "first black" partner although with his name and Caucasian features you would have to embark on a detailed genetic enquiry to know that he was of Jamaican origin.

More importantly, it was at precisely this time that I resolved that my future lay not in tax practice but in my past as a litigator and advocate.

The challenge now was how to jump down from the heady heights of City tax law practice at one of the biggest law firms in the world and still land on my feet. I knew the drop was going to be a long and painful one. The corporate clients that I had been working with at Lovells were of a completely different social bracket from that to which I returned outside the work environment. I was living a double life: by weekday I rubbed minds with the best of England in terms of education, power and earnings; by weekend I was back with my Nigerian brethren who were still feeling their way along within English society.

It was clear to me that the people in my social circle could never afford the service that we provided at Lovells and this was a key consideration in terms of my prospects of attaining partnership at the firm. For this same reason I had no list of clients at Lovells that I could claim ownership of such as would follow me out of Lovells. It was clear that I would have to start from scratch. I was like a whale that had ridden the crest of a strong wave onto the golden beach but was now faced with a life and death struggle to get back into its comfort zone.

It was now a full ten years since I had been called to the Bar and though my general legal skills were at their sharpest by virtue of the years with Lovells, I was conscious that I needed some practical experience in litigation especially as I had not served pupilage at the Bar and neither had I done the mandatory six months in litigation that all solicitors are required to do as a condition of being admitted to the Roll.

My game plan was to cash in on the kudos that I had earned from the BES litigation to ask for a transfer to the litigation department. I was confident that I would make partnership as a litigator and the plan was then to leave at the partnership level to start my own practice. My request was passed up to the Managing Partner and we had a chat about it. Yes, they were convinced of my potential in contentious matters but the problem was that good tax lawyers were rarer than good litigators. My plan had been frustrated but I understood the firm's position. So complex is the law that the big law firms have to advise on, and so short is the turnaround time allowed for them to deliver the advice, that they train individual lawyers to achieve mastery of particular areas of the law and then rely on team management to provide a holistic legal coverage.

The side-effect of this higher level of specialization is that it reduces the ability of individual lawyers to move across disciplines. The few who succeed in making any form of transition typically do so after they have achieved partnership when they have a little more control over their lifestyle. Gordon Toland, the oldest partner in the tax department and one of the oldest in the firm, was one of the exceptions. He was of a generation when single solicitors could provide full spectrum coverage for their clients' needs.

I was thrown back to considering the alternative of resigning and making a renewed attempt to practice as a barrister. This course was unappealing for a number of reasons. The principal one was financial. Although getting pupilage and tenancy in a top set of chambers would not be a problem, it was still the case that pupilage was unwaged. I now had a mortgage, two children and a wife who, herself, was still locked out of legal practice at this stage.

I had also learnt enough about the working relationship between solicitors and barristers to know how much a successful practice at the Bar depended upon the barrister having a good network of solicitors with the power to send him instructions. As with clients and solicitors, such networks are to a significant extent the product of social relationships. You may be the best lawyer in the world potentially but it counts for nothing unless you have cases to demonstrate your skill and ability.

I was clear in my mind that in the life that lay ahead of me I had to have maximum control of all the variables. I had to be the driver. In any case I had picked up many valuable skills as a solicitor, not least the essentials of seeing law as a business much more than as a profession.

It offered the opportunity to enjoy the best of both worlds by combining my aptitude for contentious work with the City experience as a transactional lawyer. This total law approach appealed to me greatly not least because it was the model that law firms in most of the rest of the world used.

If at all my resolve to do the legal equivalent of a bungee jump from the City was wavering, I was pushed over the edge by an article that came out in a legal magazine, *In-Brief,* around this time.

"Go on, put your name on the door" the headline screamed.

It was a feature on lawyers who had gone on to set up their own law firms which were now established names within the legal profession. There was David Freeman who started the City firm DJ Freeman and there was the remarkable story of Simon Berwin who had started not one but two major law firms: Berwin Leighton and S J Berwin.

I first thought of "Ogunetimoju & Co" on the door but then I thought, "Maybe not!" Based on the problems that I had experienced with that name in England, getting instructions was going to be just as difficult as getting into the legal profession. I needed a name for the practice that would neither compromise my integrity nor make the practice unviable. That name was OGUN Solicitors. It sounded right and it was me. It only remained for me to clear the use of the name with the Law Society.

I was a little concerned that because the Ogun pre-fix is quite common amongst my people and because many of us read law, someone else may have had the same thought and got in ahead of me. There was a Ogunfeibo & Co but, to my relief, no Ogun *simpliciter.*

By this time my mind had switched out of tax and out of practice at Lovells. All my thoughts were geared to my exit strategy. Part of that strategic thinking was to make the most of the training opportunities at Lovells.

The great advantage of the mega law firms is the wealth of practical legal education that is available within them. The economies of scale that they enjoy means that much of their continued professional development (CPD) training can take place in-house.

Whenever questions were asked as to what I, as a tax lawyer, was doing in CPD training sessions for Intellectual Property or Employment Department, my answer was like the one given by "the big bad wolf" in the children's fairy tale Goldilocks and the Three Bears:

"All the better to advise you on the tax implications of what you do".

This was the crash course that I took to prepare myself for the challenge of establishing the first black-led commercial law firm in England. ▨

9. BACK
II LIFE

I had resolved to jump before my 35th birthday. Even though I had only been in legal practice proper since the age of 29 having spent so much of my time on the road to commercial law practice, still the jump could not be put off any longer not least because of political developments back home in Nigeria.

Nigeria's Afro-beat artist, *Fela*, had in his song *Teacher Don't Teach Me Nonsense* highlighted some of the bad practices that the British colonial government had introduced to Nigerians. The worst, because it has carried the gravest and most enduring consequences, was the interference with the outcome of Nigeria's first democratic elections.

General Ibrahim Babangida had overthrown the administration of General Buhari in a palace coup and, to buy the support of the Nigerian people, he had promised us freedom from Buhari's 'War Against Indiscipline'. Little did we know that it was the road to anarchy that he was setting the country on to. Having, on 12 June, 1993 organised what is acclaimed to have been the freest and fairest elections in Nigeria's history, he decided to consult the instruction manual on how to override the expressed preference of the people and then proceeded to summarily annul the results of the elections for no other reason than because it produced the wrong winner: a Southern Nigerian. The political stalemate between North and South that resulted from this new exercise in the perversion of democracy was the setting in which the ruthless General Sani Abacha, another army general from Northern Nigeria, emerged from the shadows.

When Chief Abiola, the winner of the election, insisted on his prize, Abacha promptly threw him into his dungeons where he ultimately perished along with his mandate. When the protests of the playwright Ken Saro-Wiwa were calling too much gobal attention to the oil extractive operations in his native Ogoni land, Abacha had him hanged. By this time Nigerians were wishing they had stayed on General Buhari's path towards a disciplined Nigeria.

I found myself providing a running commentary on these events in my homeland to my colleagues at Lovells. It was getting harder and harder for me to reconcile my duty to my employers with my need to say what I wished to say on these developments in the way that I wanted to say it. Moreover I felt a sense of guilt. Here I was a product of Nigeria, a country on the bottom rungs of the development ladder, devoting the intellectual abilities that I had to the service of corporate Britain, a country that already enjoyed an embarrassment of riches in intellectual capital.

Though I wasn't to blame for my country's predicament I felt I had some responsibility to do whatever I was able to do to help lift it out of the mire. I had to carve some time out of the pursuit of a livelihood to make time for the work on the political front.

The Masters of the Universe

It was earlier in 1995, while I was still at Lovells in body, although my spirit was somewhere down the runway towards my great adventure, when a chance encounter occurred on the London Underground. It was to give me a peep behind the curtains on the workings of democracy in Nigeria and it was to give U.S. law capability to Ogun Solicitors within its first year of operation.

The Northern Line was, once again, living up to its reputation as the "Misery Line" on my way to work that morning. I had already boarded the train at Finchley Central when the suspension of the service was suddenly announced and we were directed off the line onto the bus service. It is on these occasions when they have a shared grudge against the public transport service that London commuters break their habit of not talking to each other.

I got talking to a slightly lanky fellow with an Irish accent who had been sitting next to me on the train. I was pleased to learn that he worked in the commercial department of the U.S. Embassy and he was pleased to hear that I was a lawyer at Lovells. We exchanged details and agreed to arrange a luncheon with our principals.

The venue was the partners' dining room at Lovells. He had invited his boss, Cantwell Walsh, a commercial attaché at the Embassy and I had invited Philip Gershuny, the partner who I considered to have the best inter-personal skills amongst the partners in the tax department. The high quality of the food matched the quality of the discussion.

When the discussions touched on the current political developments in Nigeria I must have said something that caught Cantwell Walsh's attention because not long afterwards he was putting me forward for his government's International Visitor Program. The program, he explained, was for those whom they considered were likely to have some kind of role in the countries in which his government had an interest. The program, which was funded by USAID, involved an all-expenses-paid trip to the USA for up to four weeks.

The deal was simple enough. The U.S. Government would fly me to up to six states, New York and Washington being mandatory as the power base of the government, with the rest being of my choosing. At each location they would arrange meetings with anyone I wished to meet. The quid pro quo was that I would make myself available for anyone they wanted me to meet. It sounded a fair enough deal to me and so off I went, in the autumn of 1995, to New York, to Washington and to Seattle, Boston, Tulsa, Oklahoma and Charlotte, North Carolina.

In New York I met the U.S. counterparts of the Law Society and the Bar Council where we discussed legal education and I was taken to the UN headquarters. In Washington I was taken to the U.S. Supreme Court where I posed for photos in the high-backed leather seats of the top judges in the U.S. I found the court room much more congenial than the committee room at the House of Lords that served as the court room for the Law Lords in England.

The name of each justice being written on the back of each justice's chair, I chose the chair of Justice Clarence Thomas, the sole black member of the Supreme Court. I was glad that it was only his chair that I met and not him because I was later to learn that our political philosophy could not have been more different. Even so, that a full black like me had a seat in the highest court in the land in America did reinforce my view that it was the traditions of England, and not the ability of the black lawyers in England, that accounted for the absence of a pure black judge, even at the level of the High Court in England.

Washington was also where I came face to face with the "Masters of the Universe".

Donald Easum had been the U.S. Ambassador to Nigeria in the mid-1970s at the time General Olusegun Obasanjo first came to power in Nigeria on the back of the assassination of General Murtala Muhammed. Easum had since retired to devote his spare time to charitable work in West Africa in the area of river blindness while Obasanjo had retired to his farm as a chicken farmer. Both, however, remained in contact through the Ford Foundation.

Donald Easum was one of those who had expressed an interest in meeting me. He turned up at my Washington hotel, at the pre-appointed time, in his cream coloured linen suit and crisp white shirt, and took me on a tour of the stately home of George Washington, America's first president.

As the two of us strolled in the grounds of the former home of the great American president on this sunny autumn day he pointed out, as if by way of confession, that George Washington had owned slaves and it was believed that he had fathered a child with one of his domestic slaves. Quite how the conversation moved across to Nigeria I cannot recall but when it got there I remember him asking:

"What do you think of Abacha's self-succession plans? Do you think he will get away with it"?

The new vogue from the Masters of the Universe was that military dictators *"were out"* but military dictators who were ready to leave their uniforms at home *"were in"*. The formula had been successfully tested in Ghana with Flight Lieutenant Jerry Rawlings and would be used later in Uganda with General Museveni and in Pakistan with General Musharaf.

In preparation for his metamorphosis Sani Abacha had, by military decree, promulgated a new constitution that permitted five political parties to contest the presidential elections and had got all five parties to adopt him as their sole candidate for the presidency.

"I can't see it working", was my reply.

I elaborated that as a military dictator Abacha could very much do as he pleased, but that once he took the uniform off and held himself out as a civilian democratic ruler, he would be hounded by the world media over the continued detention of Chief Abiola, the winner of the elections that Abacha's military predecessor (General Babangida) had aborted.

I added that I could not see him releasing Abiola to avoid this problem because Abiola would insist on his mandate and at the same time I could not see Abiola accepting to leave his dungeon without his mandate. A hard divide had formed with Abacha being seen as the flag-bearer of the North and Abiola being seen as the champion of the South.

"In these circumstances", I said, *"I cannot see a soft landing"*.

"Supposing the two of them weren't there" was the follow-up comment, *"who would you see as a possible successor?"*

The import of this casual hypothesis was lost on me at the time. I proceeded to explain that given the seriousness of the standoff between North and South I could not see a direct return to one-man-one-vote democracy. I speculated that there would have to be some form of transitional government, possibly a government of national unity. I proceeded to throw up some names from the different competing power sectors in Nigeria that could be pulled together to form such a government.

The one name that I did not mention was the one that the Masters of the Universe had in mind: General Olusegun Obasanjo, the former Military ruler turned chicken farmer.

"What of Obasanjo?" he said, *"what do you think of him?"*

I began by offering my apologies for the fact that I didn't have much knowledge of the man. He had been a military ruler from 1976 to 1979 following the assassination of his boss, General Murtala Muhammed, at a time when I was a political ignoramus. I explained that from what I had heard he had run a relatively clean administration and, by nationalizing British Petroleum in the face of protests from the British Government, he had shown he wasn't afraid of taking on the West. I added that with him being a former military ruler he would be able to control the army so as to contain the risk of military coups and being, at the same time, a Southerner and a Yoruba man, like Abiola, his presidency would probably serve to appease the bitter sense of injury amongst Southerners. I speculated that with the North having accepted him as supreme military ruler before, they may not be adverse to him as a compromise candidate.

"Yes, now you mention it I can see him being able to hold the fort", I concluded.

Then the conversation moved away from Nigeria.

This trip was an important contribution to my realization that I had some role to play, however marginal, in the political affairs of Nigeria and to my conviction that that role was not compatible with my duties as a City lawyer.

I never saw Donald Easum or Cantwell Walsh again but what I did see was that about three years after this discussion, on 8 June, 1998, to be exact, Sani Abacha died suddenly. It was said that he died of a heart attack. Then, just as everybody in Nigeria, at least everybody in the southern parts of Nigeria and many in the north, were jubilantly expecting Chief Abiola to be pardoned, released and installed as the duly elected President of Nigeria, on 7 July, 1998, exactly a month to the day of Abacha's death, the news broke that Abiola had also died of a heart attack. The news was broken by a former U.S. ambassador to Nigeria, Thomas Pickering, who was leading a U.S. delegation to meet with the new military leadership to lobby for Abiola's release. It was explained that he suffered the seizure while he was having tea with the delegation.

Even as Bill Clinton, the then "Honorary Black President" of the U.S. took to the airwaves to reassure Nigerians that there had been no foul play, my mind went back to the question that had been posed on that sunny Autumn day in 1995 at the stately home of George Washington:

"Supposing the two of them were not there, who would you see as a successor?"

The picture that was emerging in my mind became fully formed when General Olusegun Obasanjo, the man that I had not initially given a thought to until Mr Easum mentioned his name, was sworn in as President of Nigeria a year later, in May, 1999.

The Making of a Law Firm

My meeting with Robert Lee Fenner II, a young African-American lawyer with the leading firm Ferguson, Stein, Gresham and Sumter in Charlotte, North Carolina, as part of the same arrangements proved dramatic in a wholly different way.

Established in 1964, Ferguson Stein was a leading litigation practice in the field of civil rights, criminal defense, employment, personal injury and medical negligence. In Melvin Watt they boasted a former member of the firm who went on to become a member of the United States Congress and leader of the Congressional Black Caucus. The meeting with Robert was fortuitous because I had been billed to meet one of the female partners in the firm, Geraldine Sumter.

A graduate of the Ivy League Columbia Law School, Robert was a model young black American male: athletic, articulate and ambitious. He was excited by my insight into Nigerian political affairs and I was impressed by the fact that he had spent a year in Nigeria as part of his undergraduate study program. He was even more excited about my plan to start my own commercial law firm. I had no idea at that time that he would later come to England to join the practice.

My jamboree in America was now over and as if of a sudden, 1 February, 1997, was here.

I had done my business plan: I had raised my profile within the community and I had got my mortgage in the knowledge that if I didn't do it before resigning from my salaried post, I would not be eligible again until I had three years' trading accounts. The last step was to secure an overdraft facility from the bank. I asked for £20,000 and got £10,000.

It was a short safety rope for one who was starting again from scratch but it would have to do. The rope would either hold me up or let me down; as to which one it would be the answer was known only to the gods who were giving no clues.

The launch event was in Camden Road in a new wine bar called the Lounge Lizard owned by some friends. I just had to play the D.J. role one last time so the theme tune that I chose for the launch was *Optimistic* by the black-American Gospel-Soul group, Sounds of Blackness. Although the title was perhaps tempting fate, the lyrics were most apt:

> *"When in the midst of sorrow*
> *You can't see up when looking down*
> *A brighter day tomorrow will bring*
> *You hear the voice of reason*
> *Telling you this can't ever be done*
> *No matter how hard reality seems*
> *Just hold on to your dreams"*

The entrée to this spiritually uplifting and vibrant song is a sorrowful throwback to the torment of the African slave trade:

> *"... chains, chains, Lord won't you free me from these chains."*

The song resonated with me no end. The struggle up to this moment had been a hard one and the mental chains that had held down my true spirit and potential all of a sudden seemed to bear down on me more than they had ever done. Perhaps it is the experience of most who are imprisoned, that it is the eve of their release that they are most conscious of their bondage.

Since the initial excitement of my graduation, and my call to the English Bar I had found myself having to squeeze my intellect and character into the mould of the lawyer that I had to be to make a living. Here I was now standing on the cusp of a venture that would enable the real lawyer that was Akindele Ogunetimoju to step out. I would have control over who I worked for, the type of work I did, when and how I chose to work.

I "burned the floor" with a solo dance to the launch theme in a throwback to my disco days because it is in those moments when you are lost in the rhythms that you can find release from all the challenges of this world.

When the time came for me to give my launch speech to the invited guests I found myself returning to the theme of the hitherto caged soul. There was no need for originality, only for the words that would express the way that I truly felt. Borrowing the words of Mandela, I said: *"Free at last. Thank God I am free"*.

That freedom comes at a price was to register itself with me very quickly.

I was knowledgeable in the law and I knew a lot of people but on the first day of Ogun Solicitors I had no clients, not a single one. The reason for this was the gulf between the kind of lawyer that I had been the week before at Lovells and the kind of lawyer that I now was at Ogun Solicitors.

For most lawyers setting out on their own there would be some continuity between their past and their future such that they would be able to move into their new practice with a few loyal clients. Mine was to be a cold start from literally a blank sheet of paper. The reason was twofold: the size of the law firm that I was moving out from and the area of law that I had been practising in.

Lovells is one of the top law firms in the world. Its clients are major league global corporations whose legal services requirements are as deep in terms of technicality and detail, as they are broad in the sense of being cross-disciplinary. The technological and manpower resources required to service clients at this level are such that few law firms can offer.

To compound the matter, the tax lawyers in such a major law firm, although playing a critical role, are really but adjuncts to the main service. Tax lawyers have an almost parasitic relationship with other lawyers and do most of their feeding off the client relationships of those others. As such, a tax lawyer is the least likely to leave a secure environment to attempt to develop a general commercial law firm (as opposed to a niche tax practice) as he is worst placed to have any client following.

The phone rang once on that first day. It was my mother calling to check up on me.

It looked as if things were about to take off seriously when the next day I got a call from Andrew Gamble, a banking partner at Lovells, with a referral, a client that he didn't want to take on. Thomas Kubi was his name, a Ghanaian.

Mr Kubi had been awaiting my call.

"Aah, my brother", he said. *"I was so happy when they said you are a fellow African"*.

Since, at this stage, I was practising from home I was only too ready to agree to travel down to his office on High Street Kensington. The referral having come from Lovells, and Kubi's business address being on the up-market Kensington High Street, it was looking good.

I had managed to equip myself with one well-tailored be-spoke suit and a top-grade pair of brogues from Church's, with the promise to myself of more as the money started to roll in. As the principal of this new emerging force in City law, I had to look the part and that morning, as I set out for the appointment, I definitely did.

Thomas Kubi's office was a functional couple of rooms in a business centre on Kensington High Street. The office though small seemed busy enough. Given that, at this stage, I had no office of my own, I had reason to respect his set up. I started thinking how well he must be doing to be able to pay his office rent, his staff and his mortgage. It all seemed so daunting to me at the time. As I waited, I mused that one day Ogun Solicitors would have an office like this.

A few minutes later I was ushered into Mr Kubi's offices. Kubi was a short, dark man in the standard Ghanaian mould, of slight build with a gap tooth and a single short horizontal tribal mark on his cheek that signaled his ethnicity.

Mr Kubi had a commercial opportunity that he was proposing to introduce to an English company. His concern was to make sure that the English company would not cut him out of the deal after he had opened up. To persuade the other side of his earnest he put me on the speaker phone so that they could hear the polished tones of his lawyer, straight out of the City.

Once we had hammered out the essentials of the deal, I went back to my home-office to draft a Confidentiality and Non-circumvention agreement. Satisfied with my work, and feeling very much the born-again commercial lawyer, I sent Kubi the draft agreement for approval before forwarding it to the other side. We met again in his offices to finalise the documents.

Meanwhile I had not discussed fees with Kubi let alone given any thought to sending him an engagement letter. Just as a footballer would rather just play than train, so I was more concerned to get the work in and done. The Law Society would have hammered me if they had known.

We did eventually get on to the issue of my charges. I proposed to charge £500 plus VAT for the job. It was well below the value of the work but then again at this stage of the venture I was grateful just for the opportunity to earn. I was charging VAT because I needed the firm to look bigger than it was. This being my first client my zero turnover was nowhere near the turnover levels at which a business is obliged to be registered for VAT but I was able to sign up for voluntary registration on the basis that I expected (more accurately hoped) that my turnover would exceed the £47,000 registration threshold.

Kubi was happy with the fee but then requested to pay £250 plus VAT first with the balance to be paid within two weeks. The alarm bells should have started ringing but since it was my first instruction, I was just pleased to be holding the cheque for £293.75 payable to "Ogun Solicitors". After all up to this point I had only ever known salary cheques.

As I saw it, I had broken my duck; it was my good luck cheque. Imagine, then, the depth of my despair when a few days later, I got a letter from my bank enclosing the cheque marked "refer to drawer".

So this is what it meant to be in business! Although in one sense it was a relief that I had had this experience so early in the life of my practice and for such a relatively small amount, yet because it was the very first instruction it was a blow to my spirit; I felt it very acutely. For the first time I felt real concern for the well being of my family.

A Musical Interlude

Fear either paralyses you or it galvanizes you. Retreat was not an option. Going back to work for someone else was out of the question. I quietly resolved that if necessary I would work as a mini cab driver to maintain my family until the practice took off. Thankfully the necessary did not have to occur as a day or so later I took a call from a lawyer contact, Henry Ellis, who I had met during my time as the Chairman of the African Caribbean and Asian Lawyers Group.

He too was a sole practitioner but that was as far as the comparison went at that stage. He was an entertainment lawyer within our community where the only vibrant sector was entertainment. On his books was a man who had become the black British icon of the age: Jazzie B of Soul II Soul. It was with reference to Jazzie's tax affairs that Henry was calling me.

This was the same Jazzie B of the sound system Soul II Soul from my early music days. He had stayed on the music path and transformed Soul II Soul into a multi-million dollar band of world renown. With dance-floor anthems like *Keep on Moving* and *Back to Life*, Jazzie had moved from a small-time Sound man from Islington to superstar life on Easy Street. In the process he had built himself his own recording studio in Kentish Town, a short distance from his Holloway roots.

Here I was, on the other hand, the small-time Sound leader who had gone ahead to pursue what many would say was the more respected path of a career in commercial law, still walking on Stony Ground Avenue, relatively speaking at least.

The difference lay not in the extent to which we were each gifted but in the nature of the gift that we were trading on. Jazzie was selling entertainment, a product whose quality can be objectively assessed so that entry barriers can readily be surmounted and whose price was well within the purchasing power of all. Even the leader of the anti-immigrant British National Party could find himself, in an unguarded moment, singing along to Jazzie's lyrics. I, on the other hand, was in the business of selling commercial law advice, a luxury service whose price was beyond the reach of most, especially in our community, even assuming that they had a need for it at all.

Moreover the quality of the service that any particular lawyer offers is hard to assess remotely, which accounted for the high entry barriers that I had experienced. This, coupled with the long years of study, and the time spent in acquiring experience, means that the gestation period is much longer than for those with the gift of music. The consolation is supposed to be that the career in law is much longer lasting than the meteoric life of a soul man.

In the course of the strategic planning for the firm, I had had to reflect on where the money was within the black community in England. It did not need all my thinking ability to know that it was in the sports and entertainment fields. What was more testing was how I was going to break into these very private circles.

I had concluded that if I was going to get in at all I would have to have a product that was tailored to this market. I had first identified the product in the course of my transition from the accountants, Coopers and Lybrand, to Lovells in late 1990 and early 1991 when I was battling with the Institute of Taxation exams.

In the course of those exams, I had come to understand the significant exemptions from U.K. tax that were available to people who, although living and working in the U.K. on a day to day basis, were not "domiciled" in the U.K. With me not being a son of the soil myself, I had had reason to take a special interest in this principle of U.K. tax law.

More detailed study of Dicey, Morris and Collin's *The Conflict of Laws* on the law of domicile, led me to the realisation that virtually all African and Caribbean sports and entertainment personalities were paying tax on substantial amounts of income and capital gains that with proper advice, could have been received tax-free.

What was also clear was that although the established personal tax advisers understood the domicile principle as it applied to those, who like me, were born outside of the U.K., they had not seen the opportunity to stretch the concept to those who were born in the U.K. and even to those whose parents and grandparents were born in the U.K.

Having identified the opportunity, I stored it away in my mind for future development. Now, in the run up to the launch of the firm, I had started to peddle the product. Henry Ellis was one of the lawyers that I had taken into my confidence with a view to his giving me an introduction to his client.

So the call came and there I was, on the 20 February, 1997, in Jazzie's studio in Kentish Town.

The reception with its soft-leather seating was airy and comfortable. The plasma screens dropping sweet rhythms from

MTV Base were to be expected. It was hard to distinguish the studio staff from the young hopefuls who were drifting in and out of the recording studio as the dress code and hair styles were all in the best tastes of the music industry. Hoping that no one was looking, I took the opportunity to slip off my tie and release a couple of buttons to tone down the "City look". It was a real "Back to Life" sensation.

After what seemed a very long wait, (although I should have known that pop star clients didn't run with the same clock as corporate clients) Jazzie's Man Friday, Andy Lewis, finally appeared to take me up to the man's office.

There was the executive desk and high-backed leather swivel chair that you would expect to see in any C.E.O.'s office in the City. On the shelves where the books might have stood, sat the CDs and LPs from which lyrical and rhythmic inspiration was drawn. In place of a sideboard there was a mounted twin-deck sound system complete with gold-rimmed 22-inch bass speakers. Where the Constables, and the replica Picassos, might have adorned the walls, stood the framed gold and platinum discs.

"Bombaclart !"
The man in the dreadlocks needed no introduction. It was I the City lawyer that had to be introduced. Henry handled it.

With a smiling salute of *"Respect"*, Jazzie gave me the floor to explain the law of domicile as I was interpreting it and how, potentially, it could be used to save him U.K. tax.

Partly because I had the ability to break complicated concepts down into readily understandable language and partly because Jazzie is a man of advanced thought in his own right, he grasped the concept very quickly.

"So tell me this", he said, *"you mean even though I was born in England and have lived all my life here from the day I was born and I have never lived in Antigua where my parents came from, I can still be domiciled in Antigua for tax purposes"*.

"Yes", I said.

"And if I am not domiciled in the U.K., any income and gains that I make outside the U.K. is only taxable in the U.K. if I bring it in".

"Yes", I said, *"in a nutshell"*.

"Bombaclart!", he exclaimed, *"To Rarted!"* he added, leaping out of his seat as he did so.

The wider implications of this crash course in U.K. tax law as it applied to high earners in his position was not lost on Jazzie.

"*I wonder if Lennox knows about this,*" he said, as he picked up his phone to call Lennox Lewis, the then heavyweight boxing champion of the world.

Ever the astute business man he then proceeded to draw up a list of all the celebrities that the concept could be sold to. As he reeled off the names, I began to reflect on how difficult it would have been for me to get close enough to these other celebrities for my product pitch, yet with a supporting wind behind the product, it was looking like a walk in the park.

I explained that we would first have to get the Inland Revenue to agree my view that he was not domiciled in the U.K. before looking at his sources of earnings to see how they could be restructured to maximise the use of his non-U.K. domicile.

"*So how much is all this going to cost me*", was the question that though long in coming, was still hard for me to answer.

However confident I felt in the soundness of my analysis, at this stage it was no more than an untested theory and I needed this opportunity to prove it. I decided to bowl low on this first trial run. It was more important to prove my product with this model client as that would make future sales easier. I bowled higher on the work to be done in using the ruling to secure tax savings.

We agreed on ten percent of the tax saved or £25,000, whichever was the greater. Again because he would only be paying from actual tax savings, it was a very attractive proposition. Even so Andy, his Man Friday, said that we would first have to run the idea past Jazzie's accountant, Mr David Sloane of D.J Sloane & Co.

David Sloane and I felt mutual animosity for what we each represented even before we had set eyes on each other. He represented the ubiquitous white adviser to the rich black talent. I represented the young black upstart-professional adviser who felt that the small pool of rich black talent should be the preserve of advisers like him.

History was on my side because the normal order of things is that people find their advisers from within their own community, much in the same way as they find their life partners. This is because man is a social animal and in the natural order of things, people live and work with their own. Thus the tendency is for most immigrant peoples in Britain and other multi-racial countries to live in clusters around a hub presented by their places of worship: Jewish people tend to live within walking distance of their synagogues, Asians live near their temples and Arabs live near their mosques.

Black immigrants, on the other hand, having voluntarily or otherwise become separated from their own faiths, and with a relatively limited experience of living as a Diaspora, they tend to live wherever they choose. This is particularly true of the more well-to-do. It is this absence of the communal glue that one's own faith provides that accounts for the less cohesive living arrangements of the black community in Britain. To the extent that we live in clusters at all, it is more the consequence of State social housing policy rather than as a product of strategic thought.

As a result, whilst most Jewish entrepreneurs, for example, have their advisors and life partners from within the Jewish community, the successful black talent is almost invariably accompanied by a white adviser and white life partner. This model of relationships has a self-reinforcing tendency which later generations tend to affirm.

I had set my business plan on following the example of firms like S.J Berwin and D.J Freeman that had built their base with their home communities before broadening out. The plan had anticipated the Afro-Caribbean community moving from the first staging post of being employees to becoming entrepreneurs and employers. It was with this prospect in mind that I had decided against adding myself to the significant numbers of black lawyers in the fields of criminal and common law and to pursue instead the relatively unchartered waters of commercial law. As far as I was concerned it was time for the caretakers like David Sloane who had been servicing my people's commercial law needs to step aside.

The eyeball to eyeball confrontation between Sloane and me took place in Jazzie's office before the three-man panel of Henry Ellis, Andy Lewis, and Jazzie as the Chairman. Sloane came out with daggers drawn. His hostility was understandable, for he had a lucrative client relationship to defend. If I was right in my analysis and prognosis it would mean that the whole structure of the tax advice that he had been giving Jazzie over the years was not optimum.

The alternative to the all-or-nothing approach that Sloane took would have been to welcome my input as a means of enhancing the tax saving possibilities for his client. He slammed the door on that option when he said:

"You don't know what you are talking about. Jazzie has never lived in Antigua; he was born here and has lived here all his life. To get non-U.K. domicile he would have to show not only that he has lived in Antigua for significant periods but that he owns a home there as well as a grave plot for his use when he dies".

With this insult, the gloves were well and truly off. It was now a winner takes all situation.

I said I would accept £500 + VAT to cover the work to be done in applying for the ruling from the Inland Revenue. If the ruling was favourable I would receive a further £5,000 + VAT and I would get the brief to develop the tax strategy to exploit the ruling. It was game on.

After getting Jazzie's full life history, I sent off my arguments to the International Division of the Inland Revenue inviting them to agree that Jazzie was domiciled in Antigua. About ten weeks later I received the response:

"We can confirm that [Jazzie B] is not presently domiciled in the United Kingdom for the purpose of income and capital gains tax".

The satisfaction of having beaten the very rude Mr David Sloane was secondary. The important thing was that my theory had been tested and proven and was now available for wider application. I had secured a valuable product on which to build the firm's development in these early years.

When I gave Jazzie the news, he quickly convened a further meeting at his studio. This time Sloane was not on the guest list. It was just as well because Jazzie spent most of the time cursing, with all manner of expletives, the name of David Sloane.

The easiest part of the whole exercise was in fact getting the Inland Revenue's agreement to Jazzie being treated as non-domiciled because I was dead sure of my analysis. I was less sure about how I was now going to restructure this star's recording contracts to take advantage of his newly realized status. Having been seen to have performed one miracle, the expectations that Jazzie and his remaining team of minders now had of me were very high. Suffice to say that with careful reading of the tax legislation, and with much sweat on the brow, I was able to make his domicile status work for him. I was more than a little chuffed to see "Dele Ogun" appear in the list of credits on the inside cover of Jazzie and Soul II Soul's very next album coincidentally titled: "Time for Change". ▓

On my call to the English Bar at Lincoln's Inn in 1985
with my sister and my mother.

10. THEN ALONG CAME A MILLION DOLLAR CASE

It looked at first like I had struck a goldmine on the first instruction after the Thomas Kubi affair. With Jazzie on my new CV. I soon afterwards had an audience with Des'ree and, not long after that, I had a close encounter of a business kind with Kanya King, the founder and chief executive of the Music of Black Origin (MOBO) awards.

It was to prove a false dawn at least as far as the personal tax planning side of things was concerned. The established advisers had too tight a hold on these big new names for them to buy into my recipe despite what it had done for Jazzie. It was an easy thing for the larger firms to say to these artistes that they shouldn't risk the recipe until I revealed the full details to them; and what would be the sense in that for me?

However, the early promise was enough for Robert Lee Fenner II, the African-American attorney from Charlotte, North Carolina, who had now come over to the U.K. to do a Masters Degree in Law at the University of London. Having seen the firm that Mr Ferguson and Mr Chambers had started become a highly successful litigation practice, he relished the prospect of being in at the beginning of this quest for the Holy Grail of black lawyers – a full service commercial law firm.

It being barely three months since I had started the practice, I couldn't really afford him. He didn't care. He was ready to eat from whatever we could kill together. It was the spirit of adventure that I was looking for. With a genuine U.S.-qualified attorney from the Ivy League Columbia Law School on board, we were a transatlantic law firm as soon as we shook hands to seal the deal. Yes, we were still operating from my home-office but the excitement of the project obscured the pathos. By the time the firm was six months old there was enough of a flow to suggest that it was time for a proper address on our notepaper. Where to go was the challenge.

City Road, London is a famous road that all Britons know though they may not all know where it is. It owes its fame not so much to being the last leg of the road that takes you from London's West End into its commercial heart in the City, but to a children's nursery rhyme which goes as follows:

> *Up and down the City Road*
> *In and out of the Eagle*
> *That's the way the money goes*
> *Pop goes the weasel.*

I happened to know that an old university friend of mine had recently joined a black accountancy practice along City Road, Greaves and Associates, and that was where we headed to begin the search.

Number 368 City Road, where Greaves was based, was one of the terraced Victorian houses not that far from the Eagle pub in the rhyme. Claude Greaves, the head of the firm, was an affable guy with a toothy grin and boisterous laughter. He had a nice set-up in this office. More importantly, he had a couple of rooms spare and we quickly came to an arrangement to share his reception and conference room. It was just what we needed. It was good enough for me to invite my former colleagues in the tax department at Lovells over for a drink and I was mighty chuffed when they did me the honour.

Now it was time to bring a proper balance to the practice knowing, as I did, that I did not like procedural matters or any practice area that was largely process-driven. Real estate practice, particularly residential conveyancing, was one such area. Yet, for a law firm in England conveyancing is a crucial area that only the big City law firms can afford to leave off their everyday diet. Not only is it the bread and butter of a solicitor's practice, especially with the English obsession with owning their own homes, but a client relationship that begins with a modest conveyancing instruction can often lead to other much more lucrative work.

Smita Shah was from the Gujarat area of India via Kenya. From her I got an insight into the structure and comparative success of the immigrants from the Indian sub-continent as compared with the African-Caribbean community. What emerged was that they were a community who had a long experience of Diaspora living. Most were descendants of those who had followed the British to various corners of the Empire as indentured servants: from Trinidad, to Kenya, Uganda, South Africa etc. While the British ran the governments of the colonies the Indians ran the shops and it was this entrepreneurial experience, and the capital that was acquired in the process, that enabled the Indian community in Britain to take over from the native-born Britons their reputation as a nation of shopkeepers.

The other critically important factor was the Hindu faith. While the African-Caribbean community, having let go of their own traditional faiths, have developed in as many divergent strands as the Christian faith that they followed, the Indian community has been largely held together by a shared Hindu faith. It is this faith that has formed the spinal cord of their social and business relationships much in the same way as the Jewish faith and the synagogue have done for the Jewish community. Spiritual as well as earthly guidance is always available in the Hindu temples. I remember one Friday night traveling to Croydon with Smita to give a talk to the elders of her "Shah clan" on inheritance tax planning. I tried to imagine the Afro-Caribbean community dedicating Friday night, of all nights, to thinking about death and taxes. I also got to understand that names like "Shah" and "Patel", which had always seemed ubiquitous, were no more than clan names beneath which existed the individual family names.

She had been two years behind me in the LLB programme at London Metropolitan University. Her good looks caught my eye then and it did again when I started bumping into her on the Northern Line from Finchley towards the end of my time with Lovells. In the course of one of those train journeys, I shared with her my plan to start my own firm and we discussed how she could support the conveyancing function. Her teleguidance was crucial in my seeing through to completion the first such instruction that the firm got. The crash course was necessary because although I was now the founder and head of a firm of solicitors in England, I had not undergone the solicitors' training.

Ordinarily a law graduate who wants to become a solicitor must pass the professional examination for solicitors, and must also undergo a two-year training programme with at least six months spent doing conveyancing and six months doing litigation work. Having come to the solicitors' profession through the unorthodox route that I did (via the Bar and the company of accountants) I had missed out on this formal training.

I hadn't received any formal training at the Bar either for that matter because, as the rules were, you got the title of "barrister" immediately you had passed the Bar Exams and had eaten all twenty-four of your obligatory dinners. However, as the Bar Council's handbook says, many are called but few are chosen. The chosen ones are the ones invited into the chambers to train as pupil barristers and who then have the right to speak and, in theory at least, to be heard in the higher courts of England. The specially chosen ones are those who, after completing twelve months of pupilage, are awarded a "tenancy" (a desk in a room) within chambers and who then have the right to earn a living as barristers after all that hard work.

With my barrister title in hand – albeit with no pupilage – I gained exemption from most of the papers that solicitors would normally have to pass. The one that I couldn't dodge was the Solicitors Accounts paper. To ensure that I wouldn't have to undergo life as a trainee solicitor, now that I had tasted the high life of a fully-fledged solicitor, I delayed the application to crossover from barrister to solicitor until I had three full years of practice at Lovells under my belt.

The hard lines that the two sides of the English legal profession have, historically, sought to maintain between themselves had always struck me as self-indulgent and unsustainable. A law firm that has developed and nurtured a client relationship is compelled to hand over the client to an outside advocate, a barrister, on the approach to the court. That this practice only holds sway in England is proof enough that the practice has as much claim to superior merit as the country's equally unique custom of cars driving on the left while almost all others drive on the right.

The hand over can sometimes be a challenge for the solicitor because the relationship between the solicitor and the client is in the nature of an oath of marriage, "till death do us part". As such, the solicitor's firm will do its utmost to nurture and preserve that relationship so as never to lose it if at all possible. A case in point was an occasion at Lovells, not long after I started, when I was ticked off by a young high-flying venture-capital partner, Marco Compagnioni, for calling "his client" without first informing him. He was being careful rather than possessive. The notice that I should have given was part of the quality control process to ensure that the client got the best possible advice at all times. It is only after the senior lawyer in the supply chain has become sure of his junior's ability to deliver to expectation that the controls can be relaxed.

The barrister's relationship with the client, and for that matter, with the instructing solicitor, is not the same. It is more in the nature of casual sex. Except in the larger firms, the instructing solicitor will typically have no first hand knowledge of the barrister and will have found him through the directory of barristers or relied on the recommendation of other solicitors who have used the barrister before. If the experience was good you may get together again; if it wasn't you put it down to experience.

The defenders of the dual system will say that the rules have changed because solicitors can now qualify as solicitor-advocates and, what is more, they can now wear the barrister's wig so as to look like barristers. But for so long as the current practice continues whereby the judges are drawn almost exclusively from the pool of senior barristers, and where the advocate must, before entering the court room, still hand in a confessional slip declaring whether he or she is "counsel" (as barristers are known) or "solicitor", the disguise of the solicitors-advocate in a barrister's garb will give no more cover then a see-through negligee.

Thus it was that I, a barrister who had served no pupilage, and a solicitor who had undergone no formal training, became the senior partner of a firm of solicitors. At the time it looked like a clever manoeuvre but looking back now, there is much that I lost out on for not having received the formal training from either side of the profession.

The hardest part of all in the whole process of converting from barrister to solicitor was my having to disclose the brushes that I had had with the law in my earlier years. Well, there was the offence of being in possession of a television without a valid television licence. Then there was the time that I had pleaded guilty to driving without due care and attention when I turned right through a no right-turn sign (it was a genuine error on a rainy night). Then there was the charge that I had faced while at secondary school of handling stolen goods – a tennis racket that I had bought from a school-mate – but of which charge I had been acquitted by a genial magistrate at Brent Magistrates Court. The magistrate was rather amused by the fact that the accused in the dock before him was planning to become a lawyer when he grew up. Peter Fisher, the partner at Lovells, who had to countersign my application to convert, also found this charge list amusing; but then he had not come to the law my way.

There was one other lawyer who the profession had left out in the cold. That was Esther, my wife. She too had passed the Bar exams, had endured the dinners and had been called to the Bar. She had done one better than me by having secured six months' pupilage in the leading tax chambers, Pump Court, even though she had no real aptitude for tax law or any real aptitude for advocacy. Though she had always been more cut out to be a solicitor, we had decided that she should go the Bar route because, even then, there was a chronic over supply of law graduates chasing positions as trainee solicitors. The thinking was that the Bar route was the better of the two seemingly impossible paths to legal practice because at least by your own efforts you could assure yourself of the professional title. For those who went down the solicitor's path it was an all-or-nothing gamble because unless and until you found and completed your two-year training contract you had no professional title. However, now that I had smuggled myself behind the profession's high surrounding walls, I was in a position to let Esther in as well.

With Smita and Esther looking after the property practice and Robert and me taking care of business on the litigation and company commercial practice, we were ready for any instruction that came through. Combining, as we did, solicitors work and advocacy capability, we were justified in adopting the slogan *A New Kind of Law Firm*. The name Ogun@Law that we adopted as a play on my barrister-at-law title became very popular in the community.

We hadn't been long at 368 City Road before we had to start looking for a new office. Greaves and Associates had been forced to give us notice to quit because the landlord had become aware of our presence in breach of the terms of the tenancy agreement. He had read one of my political letters in *The Times* newspaper (when that newspaper still published the address of contributors to the letters pages). Fortunately Smita found a place just up the road at 391 City Road. This new office had a small City feel to it in that it was fully air-conditioned and self contained. We spent some money converting it from an open plan arrangement to four rooms that could seat up to seven people in total with a large conference room.

The timing of our eviction from the office share with Greaves was fortunate because by this time we were beginning to feel slightly uncomfortable with the cash-filled brief-cases that had started appearing, from time to time, on Claude's desk. He would later be prosecuted for financial fraud and Greaves and Associates, which was, when we started, the second largest firm of black accountants in England, would be no more.[1]

Asysted Development

More good fortune for our operation was to follow from a call from my old colleague at Coopers & Lybrand, Sid Singh. Some clients of his were looking for a law firm that could act on a company acquisition and he had mentioned me to them. He warned that they were white South Africans but he felt that they were the nice type. Despite the assurance, and the earlier encounter with Sir Sydney Kentridge, I was still apprehensive about how these white South Africans would cope with this black lawyer handling this important corporate acquisition for them.

It so happened that we dealt with all the early stages of the acquisition over the phone without setting eyes on each other. This was by the accident of events rather than by design because it was an information technology company for whom face-to-face meetings were a luxury to be indulged in only when absolutely unavoidable. For this reason the first time we were to set eyes on each other was on the day that had been set for completion.

As I got out of the taxi outside their offices near the House of Commons I said to myself: "Here we go again" preparing myself for the look of surprise. I passed the lawyer for the sellers by the lift lobby. I knew it was him because he was dressed like a lawyer, as opposed to a person in the IT industry; but I clearly did not register with him in the same way.

The lift took me up to the offices of Asyst International, Ltd where, at the reception, I asked for Sue Keatley or Kevin O'Brien as I had been instructed to do. Sue emerged with eyes twinkling and hands outstretched in greeting. She was an even warmer personality than she had seemed on the telephone; her husband, Kevin O'Brien, every bit her match in spirit. Once again my pre-conceptions about white South Africans had been thrown into a muddle. There was no time to dwell on the thought as I was ushered into a room where my opposite number, whom I had passed in the lobby, was already seated. Following a short introduction, Sue and Kevin left the two lawyers to do the business of getting the documentation finalized in readiness for the completion formalities.

I was to do a few more corporate acquisitions for Sue and Kevin and we became the company's solicitors. I also handled the management buyout for them when the time came for them to exit back to South Africa a few years later. Their return to South Africa marked the beginning of a deeper friendship between our families. We were later to stay with them at their homes in Johannesburg and Scarborough village, near Cape Town, when I took the family to South Africa in 2005.

Scarborough village was a quaint and serene setting near the very bottom of the continent of Africa. With the sub-zero winds blowing up from Antarctica and with us being the only blacks in the neighbourhood, you would need some convincing that this was an African village just like my own Aiyede. It could just as well have been Broadstairs in Kent, England. Cape Town itself was a marvel as to what the white leaders had done with Mother Africa (at least in the areas they chose to settle in) while black "leaders" on the continent have been content to allow it to be ravaged.

Once upon a time black Africans had lived in the Scarborough area although how their faces were not peeled by the chill winds is a mystery to me. But these blacks had been moved out and resettled to less choice parts during the days of apartheid. Now the area was home to the white tribe of Africa who had turned it into a 'Peter and Jane' picture story book setting. It came complete with a nicely secluded community beach where the neighbourhood dogs could be taken for a dawn run. From the party that Sue and Kevin threw for us and to which their neighbours were invited, I got a sense that not all were as approving of the new rainbow nation as our hosts were. I also came to understand the challenge that land reform would present when the descendants of the black Africans who had been re-settled out of the area would now have to pay full market value for a home in Scarborough village, the land of their fathers.

Meanwhile 2002 had proved the firm's leanest year. The celebration of the five-year milestone on 1 February, 2002, was a subdued affair. In truth there was no celebration. Robert and I simply shook hands and embraced in a manly hug. Two black men, one African, the other

African-American, had struggled together, since 1997, trying to build a law firm in the capital of Old England. The one shaped by the experiences of the British Empire, the other shaped by the influences of the British slave trade. Together we had laboured to persuade the British mainstream to buy our expertise in the commercial laws of England in competition with English firms who were playing the game on their home ground and who had been established before de-colonisation and, in some cases, before Abolition.

It was always going to be a tall order and so it was. Particularly as I had, from the outset, resolved that we were not going to touch legal aid (state-financed) work on which black-led firms traditionally depended. Our pride had a price. Though we played it by the book with a nice office, well put-together brochures, and first class inter-personal skills, yet the breakthrough proved elusive. We knew that the world of business runs on relationships, and we worked hard on trying to build them. The reality was that we were simply not in the loop and there was no obvious way in.

The large private corporations already had their pool of established advisers and the way in to that pool was not sign-posted. On the rare occasions when the company secretary or head of the legal department was black, our initial optimism quickly turned into graver disappointment. We found that there was greater chance of our being let in by a white "head of legal" or company secretary than a black one. We initially put this down to the oft spoken of (within the black community) black unwillingness to help their own. I later came to sympathise with the blacks in these positions as I realised that the appointment of a black firm, by a black head of legal affairs, would immediately raise questions (regardless of the ability of the firm) in a way that the appointment of a white firm would not. The simple reason was that white firms and white lawyers are the norm in England and anything else was extraordinary.

There were of course the odd exceptions that would prove the rule. These were usually to be found in the public or quasi-public sector where the organisations' funds came from public sources and the black executive, in a position to say YES, felt sufficiently assured to say YES to his own. A good example was a plucky small black Housing Association, Pathway Housing Association Ltd, whose board understood the imperative of giving firms like ours a chance to shine. Even so, many still could not bring themselves to do so and in some cases took extreme evading measures to avoid ever having to answer the question.

While the major barrier for us in the private sector was the fact that the way into the loop was never sign-posted, in the public sector where invitations to tender were publicly advertised, there was another obstacle: experience.

At least with a private sector establishment, if you somehow managed to get close enough to the decision maker, some experience and lots of capability could get you by. With the public sector, the tender process is much more mechanical. Experience, and lots of it, was what was demanded. As a first generation black commercial law firm in England, we were always going to be on a hiding-to-nothing using this criterion because, as every job applicant knows, experience is begotten of experience and unless someone gives it to you on the basis of capability and potential, you may never have it.

This is where my *alma mater*, London Metropolitan University, did me proud. I had spotted their invitation to tender in the Law Society Gazette. As the largest single university in London with over 35,000 students, they had the same breadth of legal service needs as any public corporation. In the usual parlance, they were inviting tenders from firms with "substantial experience" in any mix of these disciplines.

Our need was great and we had nothing to lose even though I was sure that we would end up with very same "thank you for your interest" rejection letter as we had been receiving in response to other such invitations. Still I entertained the hope that I could persuade the old "Uni" to look beyond our relative inexperience as a firm and to focus instead on our capability.

The interview was with a couple of Governors and the Company Secretary, John McParland, who is a spitting image of Winston Churchill minus the cigar and the bowler hat. His great leader and look-a-like would have appreciated his sharp wit and craftsmanship with the pen. I was pleased to receive a letter from him a couple of weeks later confirming that we were to be appointed one of the three firms on the panel of legal advisers that the University retained.

Even so, the mainstay of our client base was the black community. After all, one of the key planks of my original resolve to step out and have a go at building a commercial law firm was my projection that the next stop for the black middle class in England, who were presently in well-paid jobs, would be their own businesses. The problem was the short term one that commercial law is an expensive service and there were not that many in the black community who could afford it and those who could normally preferred to show it by using a mainstream firm.

Our other clientele were those of our community who were still struggling on the lower rungs of the ladder of progress. There was never any shortage of ambition here. What was lacking sometimes was a reality check particularly of a financial nature. Fantastic commercial projects, with fantastic financial projections culminating in an early float on the stock exchange, would be conceived without a basic budget having been set aside to cover the legal and other advisory costs to get the project to the starting line. To me it was a sign of mild insanity.

And then Odinma called

For all these reasons, we had struggled to achieve lift-off and shortly after the fifth anniversary date, Robert broke the news to me that he had had enough. He was getting out of the firm; out of law; and out of the country. His departure date would be the end of the current financial year, 31 January, 2003.

I learnt a lot from Robert about the African-American community over the five years that Robert and I worked together. I got to understand the rules of American football, especially the brain work that lies behind every move and why it is so like a military campaign – what you see on the field is the screen but behind that screen is a sophisticated memory chip into which one hundred and more team manoeuvres and configurations have been programmed and encoded. The best team is the one that best decodes the opponent's manoeuvres whilst pulling off its own under the supreme command of the gum-chewing head coach. I came to understand the link between college football and college education from the time he used to play the game for his college team. I got to understand the U.S. education system and the challenges that African Americans face in advancing themselves in the land of opportunity and he helped me to reconcile the images of the successful blacks in Ebony magazine with the majority black prison population in America. He even told me to watch out for an African-American senator who he said had delivered a major speech at the last Democratic Party Convention. I had forgotten the senator's name until he became famous for having the audacity to paint the White House black.

In return I shared with him what I knew about the politics of Africa by which he was fascinated. He came to understand how, though Esther and I were "Nigerians" through the design of inherited colonial boundaries that had thrown her Igbo people and my Yoruba people together as one country, we could only communicate through the colonial English language since there was no shared language called "Nigerian". He was miffed to learn that when I crossed the colonial boundaries westwards into the Republic of Benin, I could not communicate with the people there in English because they, having been a French colony, were French speaking, but we could communicate in the same Yoruba language.

It was through him that I got a sense of the loss that the thinking African-Americans feel for the land of their fathers. On one occasion when I was tiring of attending our monthly *Ikale* clan meetings he said something which touched me deeply:

"You don't know what I would give to know which part of Africa I come from. You don't know how lucky you are to know your village."

On another occasion he had spoken of the sensation he had experienced when walking around the University campus at the University of Nigeria, Nsukka, during the year that he had spent there:

"I realized that provided I kept my mouth shut and didn't say anything, everyone around thought I was one of them and it felt great!"

Robert's determination was to marry a Nigerian and, true to his character, he fulfilled his dream.

It was in the run-up to Robert's departure that we received a call from Odinma (not his real name). We had acted for him some years previously when our conveyancing team had helped him to buy his London penthouse. Those had been happier times for him in his business. Now he and his business were in trouble – big trouble. He had, through his company, been acting as the representative of a major U.S multi-national that was active, in a big way, in Nigeria's petroleum sector. This was major league – this was Enron level.

A defining feature of the Nigerian economy, and indeed the economies of the countries of Sub-Saharan Africa generally, with the exception of South Africa, is the arrangement whereby local companies and indigenes act as local representatives for foreign corporations doing business in Africa. The representative's role is to act as a pathfinder and public relations officer for the foreign entity. He is the eyes, the ears, and the voice of the alien adventurers on the ground; he will vet all tender documents and communications to ensure they are tuned for local sensitivities. Since business in these developing countries is still heavily dependent upon relationship with government, the best representatives are those with powerful political contacts who can, through these contacts, make things happen or, where necessary, make things that happened "unhappen".

For this service, the alien company will pay the local representative a percentage of the income generated from these representative services. The usual formula is "pay-when-paid" i.e. the representative will only receive his remuneration for the work that he is doing for the alien corporation when the latter strikes gold. The consolation for the representative is that when he does get paid, what he gets is substantially more than what he would have got as an employee. The obvious risk in the "pay-when-paid" formula for the representative is that it promises lots of jam tomorrow in place of a little jam today and the scope for the alien corporation to scam its local representative is substantial as is the temptation to do so. As always in business, the success of the arrangement depends primarily on the integrity of the parties but the human condition is such that integrity is rarely a convenient companion of those in pursuit of profits. Since integrity can never be assured, the next best aid is a well-drafted agreement and a supportive legal environment in which to enforce the agreement.

Where integrity is in short supply, the main exposure for the representative is that he has little or no independent means of knowing what the alien corporation receives as income from the contracts or when the alien receives it. Even where he has this information, ensuring that the alien corporation pays over what is due can be another challenge. These exposure areas should ordinarily be covered in the contract but more often than not aren't.

Sometimes this is due to the short-sightedness of the representatives. Rather than buy themselves a little up-front protection by engaging a lawyer to review the agreement for them, the sweet aroma of the ten percent that they have been promised leads them into a naïve faith in their alien business partner. Penny-wise and pound-foolish, they sign the agreement that is put before them only to discover its meaning and implications when things go wrong, at which point they have to spend much more money to salvage their position. However, even in the cases where the local representative has sufficient presence of mind to engage a lawyer before signing, the inequality of bargaining power between the parties may leave the alien company in a position to dictate the terms of the deal. This is particularly so in the developing world where wealth opportunities are limited such that there is no shortage of "others" who are ready to play if the preferred candidate gets too difficult.

The agreements that Odinma had with the American oil sector giant bore all of these features: the wisdom with the penny, the folly with the pound as well as the inequality of bargaining power.

The American company (for the purposes of this story called the U.S. Big Boys) was in the business of providing services within the Nigerian petroleum sector to the major oil companies in Nigeria: Shell, Exxon-Mobil, Texaco, Agip and the Nigerian National Petroleum Company (NNPC). The chain of production and supply from the oil wells in the troubled Niger Delta area of Nigeria to the petrol stations in the West is a very long one and there are multi-million pound contracts to be won all along the line. The U.S. Big Boys were in the business of winning as many of the competitive tenders for the supply of support services as the oil majors put out. Winning these tenders required technical expertise as well as local knowledge. Local knowledge had become especially important following the Nigerian Government's decision to increase indigenous participation in this lucrative oil sector by giving the NNPC more teeth. It was Odinma's role to provide that essential local knowledge and it was a role that he performed creditably. He had every reason to perform as he did because under the agreements that he had with the Americans, he was entitled to five percent of the "net revenues" that they received.

"Oyinbo 419"

The balance of power in these agent/principal contracts is never static. Once the agent has opened up the market for the alien principal, all but the most principled of principals begin to think that the agent is being over-compensated for what he does and they begin to regret that they had not simply taken the agent on as an employee on a salary. Such musings may lead the chief accountant back at HQ to start running the figures to show what the results would look like if they could somehow "lose" the local representative. Once the possible has been illustrated, the chief legal officer may begin to critically review the written agreements to find a way out of the contract which now, with the benefit of hindsight, seems to have been far too generous to the local representative.

In Odinma's case, the first step the U.S. Big Boys took along these lines was to get him to drop his commission rate down from 5 percent to 3 percent. This they achieved by a simple confidence trick. They pointed out to him that at present he only represented them in two of their three divisions and, even then only, on an ad-hoc contract-by-contract basis. If he would accept a commission rate of 3 percent they would make him their sole representative in all three divisions for all their work.

A reduced percentage of a much larger bowl of soup and *gari* sounded like a fair deal to Odinma and he accepted the proposal. He was sufficiently savvy to ask for the new terms to be put in writing. The U.S. Big Boys assured him that the contract was being prepared and he would have it soon but meantime there was work to do. Since trust is the best lubricant for business, Odinma proceeded to work on a number of new tender opportunities for the U.S. Big Boys. After a decent interval, so as not to come across as suspicious, Odinma again enquired about the progress of the new contracts. Again the U.S. Big Boys told him not to worry and that the draft contract would soon be sent to him. It never was.

To make matters worse, the Americans had for some time now stopped paying him even the lower 3 percent rate of commission. According to them Group HQ had given instructions not to pay him any more commission until the U.S. Department of Justice (DOJ) and the Securities and Exchange Commission (SEC) had completed their investigation into their Nigerian operations. What they were investigating in particular was Odinma's role as an alleged conduit for the payment of bribes to officers at the Shell-NNPC joint venture in order to win tender contracts.

The allegation had been made by a former employee of the U.S. Big Boys on his return home to America apparently as an act of vengeance following the termination of his employment. The Americans assured Odinma that they knew the allegations were baseless but said that there was nothing they could do until the investigation was over. They told him that his money was safe with them but that they needed his help to respond to the SEC and DOJ enquiries to enable the investigations to be concluded quickly so that they could release his money. As a token of their good faith, they offered to pay US$1 million into a neutral account, as a down payment on the commissions due to him, which sum would be released to him immediately the investigations were concluded.

Odinma, still trusting, agreed to give the Americans all the assistance that they needed, and he proceeded to do so even though they still hadn't sent him the draft contracts they had promised. They sent him a detailed "information request" that covered everything from his own bio, to staff CVs, to every aspect of his company's operations including the activities of associated companies.

An experienced lawyer would have noticed that the volume and range of the information being requested would only have been appropriate if the Americans were looking to buy his company, but Odinma had decided that the law degree that he had done some years previous was enough to see him through these multi-million dollar agreements and he wasn't going to waste money on legal advice. He proceeded to bare all.

After he had handed over all the documentary records, he was invited to a meeting in London to go through the data that he had provided and to answer some supplementary questions from the Americans' external legal advisers. The meeting turned out to be an interrogation conducted by a five man legal team from Baker & Botts LLP, the U.S. Big Boys' external corporate law legal advisers. Once the Americans had reviewed the transcript of the interrogation and the data that Odinma had provided, they sent him a further request for information. The main focus of the new information request was financial. They wanted all the financial details of the company through which he was providing the representative services and the same details for all other companies and businesses owned by him. They wanted everything, right down to petty cash receipts.

Though by now he was beginning to have misgivings over the extent of the information that the Americans were asking for, his greater concern was to bring the whole investigation to an early close so that he could get his money. The financial impact on his business had become critical since they had stopped paying his commission more than a year previously. Besides, it was too late to turn back now.

So, once more, he got his staff to down tools on all other matters and to gather together the information and records that the Americans were requesting. He had couriered the data to the U.S. Big Boys in August, 2002 and they had written to him to acknowledge receipt. In the letter they had said that they would go through the information and let him know if there was anything more they required.

It was now November, 2002, and despite his efforts to chase his commission payments, the Americans were still not giving him anything concrete. At the same time they were still asking him to work on projects on which they were making money while his money was still tied up. This was the story that Odinma brought to us in November, 2002.

Zero-Tolerance Of Bribery

I had asked Robert to take the meeting because of the U.S. law issues that I anticipated would arise from the SEC and DOJ investigations. Odinma came to the meeting with his former legal assistant whose job had become one of the casualties of the cash flow crisis brought on by the U.S. Big Boys' withholding of his commissions. I was sitting in on the meeting in case there was any insight that I could bring to what appeared to be a big case. It was just as well that I did.

Odinma was a man who used far too many words to tell a story. Of the many that he used on that day, the words that grabbed my attention were what he said the Americans had said when they received the second tranche of data from him: "We will go through what you've provided and we will come back to you if we need anything more". I asked whether they had done so and his answer was "No".

Robert's U.S. law training was extremely useful in giving us an appreciation of the work and processes of the SEC and DOJ and of the subpoenas that, we were told, had been served on the U.S. Big Boys by these U.S. law enforcement agencies. He explained that an SEC investigation, especially into allegations of violations of the U.S. Foreign Corrupt Practices Act (FCPA), was very serious business indeed. If the allegations were substantiated, it could lead to long terms of imprisonment for the directors and officers of the company as well as to seriously punitive fines for the offending company itself. However, it now looked as if the U.S. Big Boys were using the SEC and DOJ investigations as a means of avoiding their payment obligations.

Perhaps because of his impending departure Robert was not giving the client much hope with his case. It could equally have been the reputation that had been foisted upon Nigeria as one of the bribe capitals of the world that made him think that there was no way we could win the case. After all, the contract between Odinma's Nigerian company and the U.S. Big Boys, in which the Americans had devoted five full pages to a reproduction of the provisions of the FCPA, was intended to show that they had a zero tolerance policy towards bribery.

The contract contained a very interesting "get out" clause which effectively said that if the American company "in its sole opinion" concluded that Odinma's company had either paid bribes or failed to keep proper books and records, as required under the Act, then the Americans could give notice of termination and the effect of that notice would be, not only that Odinma's company would forfeit all future commissions, but it would also be obliged to pay back all commission previously received.

Under normal circumstances I might have shared Robert's sense that the case was un-winnable because of the Nigerian factor both in terms of the incidence of corrupt practices and also the poor state of record keeping (who in Nigeria issued, let alone kept, petty cash and taxi receipts !) I didn't on this occasion and I let Robert know it by kicking him under the conference table to indicate that he should allow me to lead.

It had struck me that, whatever the other issues in the case might be, the key to the case was the strap line in the letter that the U.S. Big Boys had sent to Odinma to acknowledge the second tranche of disclosures: *"We will write to you to let you know if there is anything more we need"*. I interrogated Odinma to establish whether any such letter had ever been sent to him and he had been convincing in his reply that he had received no such letter.

The opposition was scary. The U.S. Big Boy's website boasted a multi-national company with operations in ninety countries and a US$5billion turnover in the previous financial year. Its litigation lawyers, Fulbright & Jaworski LLP, were of America's elite. With close to 1,000 attorneys it ranked as the twenty-fifth largest law firm in America.

Odinma had come to us because he was on his way down-and-out, as the Americans had locked up his money for nearly two years. In short he had no money to fund the litigation, and he was looking for us to handle the case on a no-win-no-fee basis. What were we to do? In our position, one of the crosses that we had to bear was the realisation that to get to where we needed to get, we had to hitch a ride with any vehicle that came along that was heading in the right direction. Lacking the necessary experience and resources to be able to dictate our terms we had to take chances. We had never done an arbitration, let alone an arbitration before the ultimate arbitral body, the International Court of Justice at the International Chamber of Commerce. Yet here was a case that had come straight out of the blue where the amount being fought over was in excess of US$5million.

Maintenance and Champerty

I was convinced that the case would fast-track the firm into major league territory. Even if we lost, the experience we would acquire along the way would be invaluable, especially as in the early months of the practice, back in 1997, we had missed out on an arbitration instruction from another Nigerian precisely because the client wasn't confident that we had the necessary experience. Here was a client whose circumstances were such that he didn't care about our experience and was ready to make do with our raw fighting ability. We were under no illusion that Odinma would have instructed an established firm had money been no object for him at the time.

At this stage, therefore, the client needed the lawyer as much as the lawyer needed the client. We struck a deal as to fees that we both regarded as fair. He would pay an up-front commitment fee and we would handle the arbitration on terms that we would receive our time costs at the conclusion of the arbitration if we won. In addition, and as compensation for the risk that we would not receive our time costs if we lost, he agreed to pay us 20 percent of whatever we recovered for him in the arbitration.

Under U.S. rules, according to Robert, it was open to the lawyer to stipulate for a success fee of up to 40 percent of the amount recovered in this situation and some of the contracts were governed by U.S. law. The U.K. rules governing such risk sharing arrangements between lawyers and their clients at this time were quintessentially English in their frugality.

First, the form of agreement between the lawyer and the client was closely prescribed by legislation and if it failed to conform in the minutest detail, however immaterial, the agreement was void and the lawyer could not enforce it: the client would be able to walk away from the bargain with the entire fruits of the lawyer's labour. The rules, in their original form, were impossibly unfair to the lawyer supposedly in an effort to protect the client, although the corset has since been loosened somewhat. The form of the agreement apart, under English law the lawyer's compensation for the risk taken in accepting a no-win-no-fee instruction cannot be set as a percentage of the sums recovered for the client. It can only be a percentage increase on the lawyer's normal hourly rate, and that percentage cannot exceed one hundred percent of the hourly rate.

The logic of the more restrictive and intrusive position under English law is obtuse. It lies in the fiction that law in England is a profession and not a business which is a strange proposition to maintain, when English law firms have projected their presence into territories across the globe and where their annual turnover and staff head-count matches many a multi-national corporation. But close examination will expose it as a lame excuse for a rule which simply restricts the ability of smaller law firms to be fairly rewarded on a value added basis. The larger law firms are not affected by these restrictive rules because they have no need to take cases on a contingency basis since their client base is made up of equally established corporations.

The roots of the more restrictive position in English law lie in the common law rule against "maintenance and champerty". I had stumbled across this obscure rule of olde England in the course of some research on the law of restitution that I had been asked to do in my first weeks at Lovells. It was one of those research exercises that a principal gives to a new junior lawyer to keep him occupied so as to leave the principal free to get on with his work. Since that time this rule, that prevents a third party who has no direct interest in a litigation, from providing funding for the litigation, directly or indirectly, had stuck in my mind.

It still strikes me as a rule that is the product of an unequal society that seeks to preserve that inequality in terms of access to justice. The rule means that a poor man with a just claim against a rich opponent cannot augment his resources by pledging a percentage of whatever he recovers to his financial supporter. When you consider that under English law, the person pursuing an action not only has to think about his own legal costs, but also the fact that he will normally have to pay his opponents' costs as well if he loses, this rule against "maintenance & champerty" serves only the interest of the financially stronger litigant. With this rule operating to deprive the man of lesser means of the support that he might otherwise have been able to garner for the pursuit of his claim, the fear of the costs of litigation serves as a front-line defence for those who have failed to honour their bargains.

There was no better illustration of the unfairness of the rule than this case. Money was no object on one side, even without taking account of the commissions that were being withheld from the smaller man. On Odinma's side money was the big issue that stood in the way of his path to justice.

Maiden Flight of the Blind Pilot

Being in no doubt that we were going to win, I was not really interested in the niceties of the fee agreement. Odinma's word on the success fee was all that I needed. I could hear the referee saying "let's get it on". No sooner did Odinma pay the agreed commitment fee than we started trading punches with the Americans.

The first step was to test the offer of an accelerated arbitration backed up with a $1million payment into an escrow account that U.S. Big Boys had dangled sometime previously. The proposal had been on the table for some months but their commitment to it had not been tested. Now they were not so keen on it: *"There is no need to rush the process"*, was their response. It was now clear that their strategy had, all along, been to string Odinma along. It was also clear that they were not going to settle the case out of court. They were daring us to do our worst and we had to respond robustly.

I had bought a text book on arbitration and had read, and re-read, the ICC's own rules of the game. The problem is that text books can only take you so far and, in these situations, they are very poor cousins to experience. They were long on the theory of arbitration but short on the precedents that I needed. Having never received any formal training in litigation, neither as a pupil barrister nor as a trainee solicitor and with only the limited learning-on-the-job experience I had gained from County Court cases behind me, this was to be like the maiden flight of the blind pilot.

The irony was that the international arbitration team at Lovells was, and still is, the market leader amongst U.K. law firms. The team at Lovells was led by Nicholas Gould, a white-haired man in the mould of Sir Sydney Kentridge in both wisdom and humility. A year or so earlier, he had called me with a view to us acting for Texaco in Nigeria. So as not to allow the modesty of our office to embarrass our referee, we had gratefully accepted his offer to host the meeting at Lovells offices and Robert came with me to the meeting. My calculation was that with him on board as an experienced U.S. attorney, the man from Texaco would be assured that nothing would be lost in legal translation. It proved to be a mistake as Robert was a black nationalist who wore his political beliefs as an outer garment.

We hadn't quite got to the meat of the meeting when the man from Texaco mentioned a particular African-American attorney as part of the legal team they had assembled to deal with the crisis at hand. Apparently they had engaged the same attorney to manage the crisis that had enveloped the company, in 1996, following the broadcast of secret recordings of derogatory remarks that senior Texaco executives had made about their black staff. Robert could not hold himself from expressing his candid opinion that Texaco were making the same mistake as they had made before in turning to this particular attorney. A raw nerve had been touched and I winced. In the awkward moment of silence that followed I saw the instruction slip overboard and so it was no surprise when a few days later Nicholas called me to convey his regrets. The Texaco man had said he didn't feel that we had quite enough experience for the job.

In a moment of anxiety on Odinma's case I called Lovells with a view to exploring with Nicholas the possibility of the firm taking the instruction in our place but he was on sabbatical. When I thought about it afterwards I realized that it had been a call of despair borne of cold-feet because there was no way that Lovells were going to take the case without money up front. This was confirmed when, at Odinma's prompting, we now made enquiries of major law firms in the U.S.

At the American Bar Association conference in New Orleans in 1994, I had made some contacts within some of the big U.S. law firms. Vinson & Elkins was one of the biggest, certainly in Houston, the oil capital of America. I prepared a brief on the issues in the case and they came back with a quote. The fee would be between US$500,00 and US$750,000 dollars. US$50,000 would be payable up-front to be topped up in installments of US$50,000 as and when a top-up was requested. As if to make the proposal most palatable to us, they stressed that the team would include a young and very able African-American attorney. They needn't have gone to such trouble as Odinma wasn't going to be shelling out that kind of money any time soon. If he didn't know it before, Odinma now knew for sure that we were all that he had.

Still a little nervous at the responsibility I was taking on, I started thinking that the way forward was to instruct a barrister with experience in commercial arbitration in the oil and gas sector to argue the case. That would leave us free to concentrate on the solicitor's work in the litigation and reduce the burden of hope that we were carrying for Odinma. It was a division of responsibility that I found it hard to warm to. Having already identified the key to the case and with a clear strategy for arguing it, I would then have to convince another advocate of the soundness of my case strategy. Under normal circumstances it was bad enough because the credit for the successful case strategy and advocacy would go to the advocate. Here, in addition, my remuneration was dependent on the outcome. Whoever I was going to appoint had to be damn good.

Fidelis Oditah QC, SAN
The best barristers that I had any direct experience of were corporate tax specialists. I didn't really know many general commercial practitioners. Then I remembered Fidelis Oditah.

Since our paths had first crossed at the Nigerian Law School, Oditah had gone on to great heights. He had become the first black law don at Merton College Oxford, had been head-hunted from that position directly into one of the best sets of commercial barristers in the country, the Chambers of Michael Crystal QC, from where he had developed a highly-regarded commercial practice. In record time, he had become the first black Queen's Counsel in England in the field of commercial law. With his formidable legal mind, and his familiarity with how things worked in Nigeria, he was the perfect choice. The only consideration was that, like me, he had no arbitration experience. Coming from where I was coming from I was not one to put experience too far ahead of demonstrable capability.

In the decision to go with Fidelis Oditah I was mindful of the fact that all of life revolves around relationships. My relationship with Oditah had gone through a number of turns since that first encounter at Law School in Nigeria. His memory feat in regurgitating a text book verbatim in the course of the lecture had amazed me much more than my fellow students at that time since I was all too conscious of my own memory handicap. Envious though I was of his photographic memory which made studies effortless for him, my own dyslexia-assisted x-ray vision prevented me from being in awe of his legal ability and this is what led to our first encounter at the Lagos Law School being an unfriendly one.

Having been assigned to tutor those of us from overseas on the Nigerian Legal System, he had thrown a question out to the class to which no one had offered an answer. It had never been my style to be the first to answer questions even though I knew the answer. To avoid collective embarrassment I now volunteered the answer. Oditah came back with a caustic remark: *"Are you talking to your friends or answering the question?"*

I had noted that the Nigerian lecturers were in the habit of talking to their students as if the latter were children in class. One even had the audacity to tell a mature student to go and face the wall and the idiot did it. Oditah's irritation was understandable because there was a lot of chatter going on around where I was sitting but I was never one to take a slight in silence. My reply was a very British: *"If you didn't hear my answer I would suggest that you say so"*. Thus the one with the photographic memory and the one with the x-ray vision were not seeing eye-to-eye at the onset.

The relationship re-started on a friendlier footing in the U.K.. When I became chairman of the African, Caribbean and Asian Lawyers Group he had accepted an invitation to speak at one of our open meetings. Family visits followed. The two males being fairly reserved in their own ways, it was the wives and the children who developed a much warmer relationship. Against this background, Oditah was the preferred option to work with on this case and he was happy to be instructed.

In the end I decided that it would be better to appoint him as the arbitrator on our side as the contracts between Odinma's company and the U.S. Big Boys provided for three arbitrators. The decision was driven by the realisation that if I appointed him to argue the case I would have had to find another person, of like calibre, to act as arbitrator. In the end I thought the best team would be for Oditah to stand as the arbitrator and for me to conduct and argue the case.

The International Court of Justice

International arbitration is a peculiar child of international commerce, and the International Court of Justice (ICJ) is a creation of the International Chamber of Commerce. It has served the interests of big business and those concerned with cross-border trade to have an alternative forum for the resolution of their disputes which is free from the risk of national prejudices that national courts carry. The ICJ being independent of government, and having the capacity to hold its hearings anywhere in the world, represents the ultimate form of private justice for private enterprises.

Those who take the role of judges, the arbitrators, are (subject only to the overall approval of the Council of the Court) chosen by the parties to the litigation themselves. Being a private court, the fees of the arbitrators are borne by the litigants as are all the other administrative costs associated with the arbitration, including the costs of the trial centre.

In short the ICJ is like a collapsible court: the structure is assembled and erected when the dispute arises and is collapsed as soon as the arbitrators have ruled on the dispute. Since the ICJ arrangements stand independent of the territory in which it may be sited, and the parties to the dispute are typically from different jurisdictions, it operates its own unique rules of procedure. From the outset I was thrown by the unorthodox terminology.

The rules required that the claimant should kick off the arbitration process by filing a "Request for Arbitration" to be supported by a fully pleaded statement of claim. Could I find a precedent for a "Request for Arbitration?". I went through big fat treaties on arbitration law and procedure in search for a precedent for a Request for Arbitration only to later realise that what I had imagined would be a prescribed form was a simple covering letter. Relieved, I proceeded to draft the statement of case in the only way that I knew how, the style of the English Bar.

The language was tight and technical punctuated by the "on or about" and the "in or around", the "in the premise" and the "in breach of the said". When Fulbright & Jaworski filed their response I was struck by the length of the document and the simplicity of the prose complete with emotional expressions and exclamation marks. Americans have always been much more expressive than their English cousins and the pleading style reflected this. The Americans had brought a counterclaim seeking a declaration that we had been in breach and that all the contracts had been lawfully terminated by them; we were obliged to file an "Answer" to their "Counterclaim" and a "Reply" to their "Defence".

We had felt obliged to restrict our claim to the three contracts that were in writing and to leave out of the arbitration the six other contracts that were oral. This was because the law is clear that basis of the jurisdiction for arbitration is *"an agreement in writing"* between the parties in which they expressly agree to resolve their disputes by arbitration. In the absence of such a written agreement the arbitral body has no jurisdiction and the dispute must be resolved before the national courts. I had put the Americans on notice that we would be pursuing the claims under the contracts that had not been reduced to writing by action in the U.S. Courts. The strategic play that they made in response was to try to block us from this course by filing their own Request for Arbitration in which they included three of the six oral contracts as being the subject of the dispute. They then made a request for our original Request for Arbitration, and theirs, to be consolidated so as to be heard together.

The reason the Americans were anxious to have the matter dealt with by arbitration rather than before their home court is the cloak of confidentiality that arbitration offers. Had the facts of this case been presented before a court where the proceedings would have been reported, the reports would have made headline news and the unfair business practices adopted by the many multi-nationals in the course of their overseas trading operations would have been exposed. With the cloak of confidentiality, the multi-nationals are able to pick off their opponents in splendid secrecy and hence my use here of fictitious names for the parties.

It would have been open to us to object to the inclusion of the three oral contracts on the basis that they did not contain written agreements for arbitration. The Americans had clearly done their calculations as to the best ground on which to offer their resistance. Rather than dispute the existence of the oral contracts, a dispute that would have to take place in the courts without the cloak of confidentiality that arbitration provides, they had elected to fight on the substance of the agreement. It was a sensible tactical decision from their perspective because in these situations you either conduct the whole fight in the open or you do it all behind closed doors: the half-and-half option makes no sense. The bait they were prepared to use to keep the fight behind closed doors was to concede the existence of the oral contracts.

It was bait that was too tempting to pass up especially as I anticipated that we were going to have some difficulty in proving the existence of the oral agreements. Instead, because the Americans had been selective in the admissions they were making, I decided to press the concessions further.

They had admitted the smallest three only of the six oral contracts. In our answer we pleaded the existence of the three other oral contracts and requested that they be included in the arbitration. My calculation was that the Americans having opened the door to arbitration on some oral contracts, they would not now be able to block us from arguing the existence of other oral contracts that they had not admitted to but which, as we alleged, had come into being in the same circumstances.

In Memorium

The pleadings on each side having closed, it was time for the Tribunal to issue the preliminary directions and to agree the timetable for trial. The Americans had appointed Professor Bernard Honatiau, a Belgian law professor and international arbitration heavyweight, as their arbitrator. It was now for the arbitrators on each side to agree between them on the identity of the third arbitrator who would act as chairman. They settled on Toby Landau, a young star of the commercial Bar as Oditah described him. In the initial conference call between the advocates and the chairman I thought that I had heard him say that both parties should prepare a " Memorium". Again could I find a precedent for this in all the Arbitration books? I ended up exposing myself a little, to the amusement of the chairman by submitting my document as " Claimant's First Memorium" in the place of the "Memorial" that he had in fact been expecting.

The U.S. Big Boy's strategy was to prolong the process as much as possible. The excuse they put forward was the very heavy work load of Mr John Bowman, my opponent, at Fulbright & Jaworski. I was surprised that the Tribunal seemed to have no inclination to force the pace, particularly in view of the financial pressure that Odinma was under by virtue of what we said was the wrongful withholding of monies due to him.

Lacking any previous experience in the conduct of arbitration disputes I expected the process to live up to its claim as being a faster and more cost-effective means of resolving commercial disputes and, relying on its published rules, I believed that the International Chamber of Commerce, the governing body, would be vigilant and pro-active in ensuring that the case progressed quickly. In taking the rule book to mean what it said, I was showing my inexperience.

After what seemed an eternity, we finally got a timetable from the Chairman. We were desperate to get the hearing on before the beginning of August, 2004, to avoid the long summer recess that the Bar enjoy. The concern was that if the trial was to overrun the allotted days for any reason, the likelihood was that it would not resume again until October, 2004, and the case was hurting our cash flow badly.

It is in the nature of a small business with limited manpower that once the business is tied down with a large order, there is precious little capacity to do anything else. In the short term the business must draw on its reserves and pray that it makes it through to payment. If it doesn't, it goes bust. We had no reserves to draw upon as the lead-up to the case had been a very dry period. All that we had to fall back upon was our ballooning overdraft and the goodwill of our bankers. Odinma too was feeling the squeeze on his financial arteries. The contracts with the U.S. Big Boys were the key platforms on which his financial standing was built; everything else was incidental. Thus lawyer and client were walking a financial tight rope. This bonded us: I could feel his pain as he could feel mine.

Having waited so long for a trial date, imagine how we felt when Mr Bowman now requested an adjournment of that date until October, 2004, the other side of the summer recess. The excuse for the request was one that I expected to have been thrown out immediately. The story was that Fulbright & Jaworski had just been instructed on a new arbitration that was so big, urgent and important that all the arbitration partners had been instructed to put on hold whatever they were then doing to concentrate their efforts on this new case.

"As if", I thought. Surely the tribunal would see this as an inappropriate excuse. Had this been a normal court the judges would at least have demanded to see evidence of this new and sudden emergency and they would have required to be persuaded that no other lawyers could attend to the new case. In short, it would have taken a lot of persuasion before they would agree to change the trial dates at such short notice. The tribunal embarked upon no such enquiry. The truth of the claim was never questioned and the commencement of the trial was pushed back to 13 October, 2004; a full two years after the original request for the arbitration.

Odinma was devastated by the ruling and began to be concerned as to whether we would get a fair hearing given the U.S. Big Boys' apparent ability to bend the process to their will. There was, however, nothing that we could do about it now. I had booked the family holiday for August/September with a view to using it to recuperate from the stress and long hours of preparation for this case. The holiday was now going to be a working holiday being as it was so close to the trial on which so much was depending.

Let's Get It On
The trial date finally came although not without one last twist in the timetable. Our arbitrator, Fidelis Oditah, had to change his flight back from Nigeria so that we would now not be starting first thing on Monday morning as planned. Meantime the arbitrator chosen by the U.S. Big Boys gave notice that he had to leave early on Friday to catch his train to Brussels. It was looking as if the trial might not finish and matters might have to be held over after all. There was, however, no way that I was going to allow that to happen. Come what may we would finish on time even if I had to take some risks with the evidence. I prepared zealously to make sure that I was on the ball and that I was in a position to present our case with military precision.

I checked into the Hilton hotel in Islington for the week of the trial. Being eight minute's walk from the office, this would cut out the time that would be lost in travel and family interaction. Each day I would work in the office until around 3 or 4 am before walking to the hotel to catch a quick nap, a fresh-up and breakfast before returning to the office at 6.30a.m. The taxi would be booked for 8.30a.m. to take me to the trial at the International Disputes Resolution Centre on Fleet Street.

With my lone assistant, Emefa Kattah, now being away on maternity leave, and with the only other candidate my youngest sister Remi (who I had now let in through the barricades of the profession as a trainee) having child-care issues that made an early morning start problematic, I was the files clerk, the assistant and the advocate all in one. The trial "bundles" had already been lodged at the trial centre in the customary way but that still left me with ten large lever-arch files as my own set of the bundles together with three data boxes of financial records.

Mercifully, the IDR building is a modern, state-of-the-art building, with large revolving doors at the entrance and with spacious and modern lifts to take you up to the court room. Still learning on the job, I was relieved to be told by the receptionist that one of their staff would be bringing all my files up to the advocates' room. The room for each advocate was spacious and highly befitting of the status. Separating the two rooms was a consultation room in which confidential discussions could be held.

The gladiators on each side were introduced. Their team looked as impressive as it was sizeable. There was John Bowman, my opposite number. In the best tradition of American lawyers he was dressed in the national colours in a navy-blue suit, with a crisp white shirt and red tie. Tall and clean-shaven, he spoke with a classic Texan drawl. He was easily 15 years my senior in age and many more in experience in these surroundings.

With him were an array of witnesses who had flown over for the trial. From the company were the Chief Legal Officer and Head of Compliance, a Financial Director and an Operations Director. Then there was their expert witness, Mr Nicholson, an audit partner from a big accountancy firm. On our side it was just me and Odinma as the *dramatis personae* although Odinma's former assistant had come along to give him moral support.

Thus were we lined up. An all-white team against an all-black team before a black-and-white tribunal in London. We were there to resolve a dispute between an American corporation and its Nigerian business partner over contracts that were to be performed in Nigeria but which were expressed to be governed mainly by English law but with aspects that crossed into the law of Texas and in which U.S. federal law on foreign corrupt practices formed the undercurrent.

As we were called into the room before the assembled arbitrators it was all still a new and surreal experience for me. I was relieved to see that the arrangements were very informal, no gowns, no wigs, but plenty of technology. The desks were arranged in an almost horse-shoe shape in relation to the judges who sat behind individual desks. Each desk had ultra-modern laptop computers and microphones. The laptops were wired up to give near simultaneous reproduction of every word that would be spoken in the course of the trial on to the screen. This real-time transcription service freed the advocate from having to bring along another lawyer just to take notes. It was also possible for the advocate to scroll back on the transcript to check what had been said at any given time. As if that wasn't pampering enough for the advocates, we were assured that the day's proceedings would be fully transcribed and delivered to our offices within two hours of the close of proceedings for that day. This was trial advocacy in its most refined form and I was up for it.

An Old Texan Saying
As with the pleadings, the style of the Americans' opening statement was radically different from what I was accustomed to in the English courts. It had all the theatrical language that one might expect to see in a criminal trial in England but not a civil trial. Mr Bowman even managed to work into his opening a few old Texan sayings the most memorable of which was *"Judge Roy Bean was the only law west to the Pecos"*, though it left me a little non-plussed.

One thing that Americans generally have a gift for is public speaking. It is an aptitude that identifies the nation much in the same way as mathematical skills identify the Chinese. I started off admiring the controlled eloquence of John Bowman's opening as every word was accorded its own place in time. That was until it dawned on me that the best part of the morning had been taken up by his speech. I started to wonder whether we were going to be able to finish the trial given that we only had three and a half days in total.

The joy of litigation and advocacy that surpasses all other areas of legal practice is its dynamism. In our first brochure for the firm we had used sports imagery to illustrate the different practice areas. Our employment law practice was depicted by a Formula 1 motor racing pit stop which showed the different members of the team performing their individual functions and the interdependence of the whole exercise. Our tax practice was depicted by an ice hockey goalkeeper as a parody for the tax inspector with all the protective armour of the state defending a small goal.

My favourite was the boxing contest which represented our litigation practice. After weeks and weeks of preparation for the encounter, the day finally comes when the prize-fighters engage in the ring. Each brings along with him his supporters who will be rooting for him come what may. The referee, on the other hand, even if he has a hidden personal preference, must announce the victor according to the quality of the blows landed by each of the pugilists.

Any boxer will tell you that success in combat is a combination of preparation and inspiration. Just as a boxer must be physically conditioned such as to be able to draw upon his repertoire of manouevres and punches whenever necessary, so an advocate must have his core facts at his finger tips or at least know where to find them in an instant.

The inspiration bit in boxing is the brain quality that will always separate the boxer proper from the puncher. This is the Ali v Foreman and Mayweather v Hatton dimension. It comes from careful study of your opponent's strengths and weakness and, more importantly, your own strengths and weaknesses. For an advocate the case is won or lost, all other things being equal, by the quality of one's insight into the strengths and weaknesses of one's case. Having performed this analysis one then sketches out the story or, if you like, the picture. At the end of the day the victor is the one who, using the available facts, paints the most convincing picture or tells the most persuasive story to the unbiased mind.

Different Strokes

The story that the Americans brought to the Tribunal was a superficially appealing one. The Government of the United States of America, more than any other government in the world, has made clear its abhorrence of the practice whereby international business is won through the payment of bribes to government officials. The U.S. Government has sought to lead by example by taking responsibility for its own citizens and corporations by unilaterally passing into law the Foreign Corrupt Practice Act (FCPA) 1977. Under the Act it is an offence for a U.S. citizen or corporation to offer or to pay bribes to officials of foreign governments.

The interesting thing about the U.S. justice system is that it can be awesome in its independence. As the collapse of major institutions like Enron and Arthur Andersen shows, no corporation is bigger than the laws and the flag of the United States of America. Contrast the workings of the British justice system in the same area. The British Prime Minister, Tony Blair, was able to call a halt to a judicial enquiry into allegations that bribes had been paid by BAE Plc to the Saudi Government to win major defence contracts on the basis that the enquiry would prejudice "national interest". However, business being business, and in circumstances where competitors are not playing by the same rules, U.S. corporations take the view that the game must go on albeit with the exercise of more care than British and other global corporations, if only because the consequences for the U.S. corporations of getting caught are that much more dire and assured.[2]

The first step in the process when the U.S. authorities have sufficient reason to believe that a U.S. corporation has contravened the FCPA is a combined investigation by the U.S. SEC and the DOJ. These investigating bodies have power to see anything, go anywhere and to interview any person in the course of their investigations.

For a listed company, the first tremors following the service of notice that the SEC and DOJ are starting an investigation is felt in the share price. Thereafter the tremors work their way right up through the corporation to the Board as the realization dawns that such serious criminal conduct is likely to result in very stiff jail sentences. Where the evidence of violation of the FCPA is not strong enough to secure convictions, the corporation might be served with a "Cease and Desist Order" which puts the corporation on probation and warns of serious consequences if the conduct is repeated while the order is still in force.

The story that the U.S. Big Boys brought to the arbitration was that for all these reasons they took their obligations under the FCPA very seriously. This was the reason, they said, why they had taken the precaution of including as standard provisions in all their contracts provisions that mirrored their FCPA obligations. The key part of these obligations, they said, was the compilation and preservation of proper documentation, "books and records", by means of which all expenditure could be verified and audited. They supported this, they said, by conducting thorough and proper "due diligence" on all companies that they proposed to do business with before getting into any kind of relationship with them.

They explained that in order to safe-guard their position under the FCPA, it was a standard term in all their contracts that they had the right to terminate the agreement with the third party:

"immediately upon written notice in the event that the company concludes in its sole opinion that the Representative or any of its Associated persons has failed or will fail to meet their obligations". The "obligation" of the Representative was to *"make and keep books, records, and accounts which, in reasonable detail, accurately and fairly reflect the transactions and dispositions of the assets of the Representative".*

To police the Representative's compliance with these obligations, the company had reserved to itself:

"the right to access the books and records of the Representative [and] the right to have an audit done of the Representative at any time".

The story went that Nigeria and Nigerians being notorious for corrupt practices, one of their former employees, in an attempt to blackmail them into a compensation settlement, had made false reports to the SEC and DOJ alleging that they had paid bribes to officials of Shell-NNPC joint venture in Nigeria in order to win tenders. Odinma, it had been alleged, was the conduit for these payments. These allegations had led to the SEC and the DOJ starting an investigation into their operations in Nigeria as a result of which they had been subpoenaed to produce an extensive array of documents and financial records to prove that they had not violated the FCPA.

On turning to Odinma and his company to produce the documentary information that they needed to respond to the SEC and the DOJ, the story continued, they found that the he had failed to keep proper books and records as he was obligated to do under the Agreements. It was in these circumstances that they had exercised their right to terminate the contracts with the consequence that under the terms of the contracts they were freed from all further obligations to pay commissions to Odinma and, furthermore, Odinma was now obliged to return all the commissions that he had received since the inception of the Agreement.

Bowman having finished his opening statement, I was invited to call Odinma, our only witness, to take the stand. To save time his written statement was taken as having been read before I handed him over for cross-examination. Though dressed to impress he was visibly nerve-wracked. It was understandable as he had a lot at stake: he was a "Big man" in Nigeria, a country that respected only "Big men". If he lost this case he would be losing everything. He was, effectively, on trial for his life and not just his livelihood.

My Cousin Vinny

A good advocate approaches every witness with a clear idea as to what he needs the witness to say either expressly or by necessary inference from established facts. Bowman was a good advocate and he had identified alternative ways to catch Odinma. He needed Odinma somehow to admit that he had volumes of documents relevant to the U.S. Big Boy's enquiries and which he knew they had asked for and which he had deliberately withheld. Alternatively he needed Odinma to admit that he had not kept proper books and records in accordance with his contractual obligations.

The problem for Bowman was that we had a complete answer to the case he was trying to construct. Yes, we had volumes of documents consistent with our obligation to maintain proper books and records, and the U.S. Big Boys would have been able to see all these records for themselves had they chosen to exercise the right, which they had under the contract, to call at any time for a third party audit of those records. Besides, it wasn't that we refused to produce any particular records; we in fact produced all that they asked for.

Try as he might Bowman could not find a way through our defensive guard. He wasn't helped by the fact that his clients evidently did not keep any records themselves as he could not produce from his client's records a single document that Odinma ought to have had but had failed to produce e.g. copy correspondence that they might have sent to him.

In the course of John Bowman's extended cross examination of Odinma, I got the impression that the game plan that the Americans had decided upon was to play for extra time by drawing out Odinma's cross-examination in a sort of filibuster performance that one might expect to see in a parliamentary debate rather than a civil trial. If the hearing had to be adjourned, given the busy diaries of the individual arbitrators, it would probably take until late December before a new date could be found that would be convenient to all parties. The strategy, if that is what it was, would have been greatly assisted by the fact that it was never Odinma's practice to give a short answer when he could give a long one instead.

This is another drawback of arbitration as compared with the court system. Especially where, as in this case, the hearing is before a panel of three arbitrators rather than a sole arbitrator. Getting the diaries of five private practitioners, each with many other commitments, to line up can be a difficult task.

My suspicion that the U.S. Big Boys were reverting to a dirty-tricks strategy became stronger after Bowman had cross-examined Odinma about his signature on the thirtieth cheque when it was clear that the answer to the thirtieth illustration of the point that he was making was the same as the first illustration. In this way Bowman's cross-examination of our one and only witness took us to the close of the second day of a three and a half day trial leaving me a little over one day to get through their four witnesses.

As I had expected, the first witness that they put forward was Mr Nicholson, the expert auditor. The U.S. Big Boys' case rested on his standing as a very experienced auditor in one of the world's largest and most respected auditing firms, and on the expert opinion that he had formed on the adequacy of the records that Odinma had supplied. He was going to say that he had formed that opinion based on his personal examination of the records and he was going to explain to the tribunal the kind of documents that one would expect to see if proper books and records had been kept. He was also going to say that the obvious conclusion was that Odinma did not have these documents because he had not produced them.

In preparing for this case the biggest judgment call I had had to make was how to deal with Bill Nicholson's evidence. It was an issue that I had agonized much over. At one stage I thought a Nigerian accountant would be the best antidote as this would leave us scope to argue that Mr Nicholson was speaking from the wrong reference point as a U.S. practitioner commenting on accounting standards applicable to a Nigerian company. However, from my time with Coopers & Lybrand, and my experience as a U.K. corporate tax practitioner, I knew enough about the accountancy profession to know that accounting standards were fairly universal in their requirements, which is precisely what makes it possible for the big Anglo-Saxon firms to dominate the profession outside of their home bases. Nicholson had, in any event, taken care to get input from his firm's Nigerian office. Thus, the line of argument that Mr Nicholson does not understand accounting standards in Nigeria was not going to get us home.

After fretting over the issue for a while, the penny suddenly dropped and the way forward become very clear: we were not going to call an expert accountant to challenge Mr Nicholson's evidence. It struck me that that was precisely what John Bowman wanted us to do. He had chosen the accounting evidence as the ground on which he wanted to conduct the fight. From the financial records that I had reviewed it was obvious that if we were made to fight on this ground we were bound to lose as the records were simply inadequate. Besides, we didn't have to go down this road to win.

Though the Americans had sought to bury us with a mountain of financial documents, the dyslexia-assisted way of reasoning helped me to see through the detail to identify the core issue. The issue, as I saw it, was not whether we had kept "proper books and records" as we were required to do under the contract, because the U.S. Big Boys had missed the two opportunities that they had to make this "the issue". First they could have, prior to giving notice of termination of the contracts, exercised the right, which they had under the contracts, to "inspect or audit" Odinma's books and records. They could also have asked Odinma to demonstrate, to their satisfaction, that he had kept the records in accordance with the contract. Had they done either of these things we would have been in an impossible position because, in a developing country like Nigeria, most dealings are paperless.

Having missed these opportunities, and having taken the route of asking him to produce specific documents enumerated in their two letters, the core issue was whether Odinma had supplied the requested documents. There being no doubt that Odinma had provided documents and information in response to both letters, the issue boiled down to a question of the completeness and sufficiency of what he had supplied. Unfortunately for the U.S. Big Boys, in their letter acknowledging Odinma's response to the second of the two information requests, they had said that they were going to go through the material that he had provided and that they were going to write to him to let him know if there was anything more that they needed.

From the grilling I had given Odinma when he first instructed us on the case about whether the U.S. Big Boys had written to him subsequently to request anything more, I remembered that the answer was a categorical "No". Provided I could ensure that the documentary enquiry stayed on this line, I gambled that I could do without an expert witness to counter Mr Nicholson's evidence.

On a hunch, I read Mr Nicholson's statement again in the hope that it would confirm the date on which he had been instructed by the U.S. Big Boys. My hunch was that this was after the Notice of Termination had been served. I had guessed right. His witness statement showed that he had been instructed after the date on which the arbitration process was commenced. This told me that Mr Nicholson had been asked to form his judgment on whether Odinma had kept "proper books and records" solely on the documents that Odinma had supplied in response to the information request. The Us Big Boys had not asked him to carry out any investigation into the issue before they served the Notice of Termination. I was now looking forward to my cross-examination of Mr Nicholson.

I started his cross-examination by inviting him to agree that the Americans had made two specific written requests for information and documents from Odinma. I next asked him to concede that the documents that Odinma had supplied, and which he, Nicholson, had later been given to assess, had been supplied in response to these two itemised list of documents. Next he was asked to read the letters and to accept that the letters had made clear the purpose for which the documents were being required to be supplied viz to assist the U.S. Big Boys in responding to the enquiries made by the DOJ and the SEC.

From here he was obliged to admit that Odinma had not put the documents forward for the purpose of proving that he had a proper and adequate accounting system or as his "books and records". With this concession on the table, combined with the fact that he had been instructed after the litigation commenced and had never been to Odinma's offices in Nigeria, Mr Nicholson had to admit that the expert opinion that he had formed was based strictly on the documents that the U.S. Big Boys had forwarded to him completely removed from the context in which they had been provided. In other words he had been marking a different examination from the one that the U.S. Big Boys had set for Odinma.

Having got what I wanted out of Mr Nicholson in a question-and- answer session lasting little more than an hour, I was able to release him. The U.S. Big Boys' Goliath having been slain with five sharp blows from David, the rest of the army had reason to be worried. The relative ease of Mr Nicholson's cross-examination owed a lot to his professionalism; he was not about to try to bend obvious truths for anyone.

The other aspect of the financial/accounting evidence was the number-crunching to prove the amount that was actually due to Odinma. The easy bit was that the contract said he was entitled to "3 percent of net revenues actually received". The challenge was proving what the Americans had actually received as distinct from what they were prepared to admit to and then calculating the proper deductions from gross revenues to arrive at "net revenues".

The second arrow in the American's quiver of dirty tricks had been to swamp us with financial records. I had had to instruct an accountant to help me make sense of the boxes upon boxes of invoices and payment vouchers, relating to the several contracts, running back several years.

Next up for the Americans was their finance director whose brief was to ensure that "net revenue" was as low as they could possibly get away with. Her testimony under cross-examination was again straightforward and honest and therefore easy. Though she had prepared realms of spreadsheets showing "net revenues" and "commissions due" in exciting colours, it was nothing but a faithful reproduction of what her colleagues in the U.S. Big Boy's Nigerian office had fed through to her. She readily admitted that she had not herself verified the figures against payment advices or payment vouchers or bank entries. In other words, to borrow Mr Nicholson's accounting language, she had not seen the "source documents" which alone could have "legitimized" the amounts that she was reporting as having been received by the U.S. Big Boys. The deductions from gross revenue that she had made in her calculations were equally unsubstantiated because they were dependent on a number of contingencies that had not been shown to have occurred.

Finally the Americans called their Chief Legal Officer and Head of Compliance as a witness. On paper, by virtue of his legal education and experience, he threatened to be the hardest of the opposition's witnesses to break down. However, when the facts are not on your side, the more legal knowledge you have the more of a handicap it can become in the witness box. It is as if the legal processor kicks into operation as soon as the question unfolds prodding the lawyer-witness to give the logical answer while the other side of the brain tries to hold him back from doing so. The result, at least in this case, was guarded and evasive responses to questions that carried no conviction.

The Americans had first sought to run the argument that the documents that Odinma had produced were not "responsive" to their written requests i.e. that he had either failed to supply the particular documents requested or else had supplied irrelevant documents.

As part of the pre-trial directions the Tribunal had raised its concern to clearly understand each side's case in relation to the documents that were actually requested and the documents actually supplied. The Americans' original game plan had been to focus on the quality and completeness of the information supplied in response to each request to show that it was inadequate and, from there, to argue that the inadequacy was proof of the fact that Odinma did not keep proper books and records. In readiness for trial they had produced what they termed a "Schedule of Responsiveness" in which they summarised which of the documents supplied by Odinma were "responsive" to the specific documents that they had requested and which were not.

But the Schedule was threatening to become their own noose in the light of my argument that all Odinma had to show was that he had responded to each of their requests and that, if there was any issue as to the sufficiency or completeness of his response, it was the Americans' responsibility to let him know and to request more information. Knowing that their Schedule of Responsiveness showed that each of their nineteen requests had been responded to, they now sought to escape this "own goal" by not including the Schedule in the Trial Bundle. They argued that the document was legally privileged from inclusion in the bundle as it had been prepared by them for the purpose of obtaining legal advice.

It is of course difficult to fail an examination when you have got the answer sheet in your possession. If the Tribunal were going to allow the Americans to keep the Schedule out of the Trial Bundle there was little I could do about that, but there was nothing to stop me using the contents of the copy of the Schedule that they had earlier supplied in my cross-examination of their Chief Legal Officer. And so I proceeded to take him through each of the nineteen requests and, having established that he had assisted in the compilation of the Schedule, it was an easy exercise to get him to admit the documents that were responsive to each request. In this way though the Schedule of Responsiveness was kept out of the Trial Bundle its contents made it through as part of the evidence.

Taking his cue from Bowman's opening statement, the Chief Legal Officer told his version of the same story. The U.S. Government, in its position as leader of the "free world" takes its international responsibilities seriously and had taken a unilateral lead in setting moral standards for international business in removing the scourge of corruption in international contracts. That lead came in the form of the Foreign Corrupt Practices Act under which U.S. corporations may be held to account for any bribes paid in any part of the world where they may be operating. They, as a responsible U.S. corporation were following their Government's lead: *"We took our FCPA obligation seriously"*, he said. He, himself, had been recruited as Chief Compliance Officer specifically to further strengthen the company's compliance record in this regard.

The evidence, however, showed the contrary. Though they had incorporated the relevant provisions of the FCPA into their contracts with Odinma, it became clear that the provisions were there simply as additional hooks on which they could hang any claim to declare Odinma's commissions forfeit. The Americans never themselves observed their FCPA obligations. The compliance file that they had compiled for Odinma was a bare cupboard. The annual Certificate of Compliance with the FCPA provisions that they were supposed to obtain from Odinma had never been done. Although the contracts gave them the right at any time, and at Odinma's expense, to call for an independent third party to conduct an audit of Odinma's books and records, they had never bothered to exercise that right. Most remarkable of all was that the Americans kept no records of their own. All the documents that they were using to prove their case were the documents that Odinma had supplied in response to their information requests. Theirs was a paperless business philosophy based on the logic that "whatever is not written down cannot be proved against us".

Against this background the cross examination of the Chief Legal Officer, on his testimony that they took their FCPA obligations seriously, assumed semi-comical dimensions; the whole encounter was over within two hours. In this way we were able to get through the evidence within the three and a half days notwithstanding the best efforts of the Americans to play for extra time.

The Tribunal having directed that closing arguments should be delivered in writing, with each side having an opportunity to submit a further written rebuttal of the other's closing arguments, we had every reason to think that the judgment would come through fairly quickly especially as all the oral exchanges had been efficiently transcribed at the end of each day.

At Odinma's prompting, I took the opportunity to ask when we might expect the decision, reminding the Chairman that my client had been out of his commission income for over three years and that his business was under significant stress as a result. The chairman's response was a non-committal: "We have heard what you have said and we will certainly work on the decision as soon as possible".

Notwithstanding, we left the Trial Centre with a buzz that day. If Odinma could have carried me shoulder high he would have because no one who had sat through the trial was in any doubt that we had completely demolished the U.S. Big Boys' case. This was Joe Peschi's moment of victory in the film *My Cousin Vinny* all over again where the mildly dyslexic rookie upstart had vanquished the pedigree opposition.

Now the wait for the referee to announce the victor. ▨

11. ET TU?

 Four weeks passed and we were waiting. Eight weeks passed and we were still waiting. Three months passed and Odinma began to wonder whether the U.S. Big Boys were using their influence to stall the decision.

With no prior experience of international arbitration to guide us, we could not begin to see any rational explanation for the delay. After all it had been fairly obvious to everyone at the end of the trial that we had won. Furthermore the pleadings had all been in writing, as had been the opening and closing arguments as well as the post-hearing submissions. Add to this the fact that all the evidence had been comprehensively transcribed at the end of each day, what could possibly account for the delay in the Tribunal announcing their decision and giving their reasons?

With great difficulty, I persuaded Odinma to exercise a little more patience before we started querying what was going on as we did not want to get on the wrong side of the Tribunal for any reason. Another four weeks passed with calls from the client on each and every Friday, asking whether we had heard, asking for explanations, and putting forward his own theories about why we had not heard. After nearly six months had passed without a word about when we could expect to receive the decision, and with the firm's overdraft threatening to break through the extra credit limits that the bank had extended to us on my assurances of our victory, I was forced to call the ICC Secretariat to complain about the delay.

And still we waited. The ICC Secretariat proved toothless as far as the Tribunal's pace of work was concerned. The lesson slowly dawned that although the ICC Rules boldly declare that the decision of the Tribunal must be sent to the Court no later than six months following the close of the hearing unless an extension of time has been granted, the Court's habit was to grant extensions whenever they were requested by the Tribunal Chairman. Each such extension giving the Tribunal a further six weeks lease of life.

Another Fight Breaks Out

Our letter of protest against the grant of any further extensions, in the light of the already protracted time table for the hearing and the financial distress that our client had been experiencing, and the real and present danger that his creditors were threatening to force his business into liquidation, carried no weight with the Court who granted two further extensions. 10 months had now passed since the end of the Trial and we had no levers left to pull. In the meantime I became engaged in another fight for Odinma.

When times had been better he had bought himself a 999 year lease of a luxury penthouse in Central London through an offshore company. When the troubles started the service charges and the ground rent due under the lease had become one of the early casualties of his cashflow crisis. The landlord was not amused.

Having issued court proceedings to recover the sums due from Odinma's offshore company, and the company having failed to defend the claim because those who were acting as its offshore directors were themselves owed money by Odinma, the landlord had been given judgment "in default of a defence". The landlord had also in fact gone further.

Under the terms of the lease he was entitled to treat the sums due as "rent" and he was entitled to treat Odinma's Lease as having become forfeit for non-payment of rent and he wasted no time in doing so. Thus, for a debt on account of unpaid service charges and ground rent totalling a little under £20,000 the landlord was gaining a penthouse worth over £1million.

Surely this could not stand? Surely the laws of England must contain provisions that would operate to soften these hard edges of the law governing the relationship between landlord and tenant?

I was in the middle of preparation for the arbitration hearing when Odinma brought this new crisis to my attention. He accepted that my hands would be tied up until after I had submitted the Post Hearing Submissions in the arbitration. After that, I took a breather for a couple of weeks before looking at the papers on the new matter.

This was September, 2004, and I had not looked at landlord and tenant law since I studied the subject at Bar School in 1985. Even then this area had been the most technically challenging of the available optional subjects for the aspiring barristers. The layers of legislation reflected the ever-shifting Parliamentary bias between the powerful interests of landlords and the vulnerable position of tenants. This was the ultimate legal battlefield between the interests of the Haves and the Have-Nots; between the landed gentry and the commoners.

Once again, experience was against me although by now Odinma was convinced that I was a miracle worker as far as legal problems were concerned. As it turned out it was I who was looking for a miracle this time round. The two weeks spent recuperating from the exertions of the arbitrations was two weeks that we couldn't afford. The one thing that I needed to have known, and which I didn't know, was that a tenant whose lease had been forfeited had only six months from the date that the lease was forfeited to apply to the court for relief from forfeiture: once he missed that boat, the legislation provided that he would be barred from all further relief. By the time I got up to speed on this principle the relief boat had left the harbor two weeks previously.

Our opponents knew that we had missed the boat; they had made sure of it by dragging their feet in responding to our request for a settlement figure. Now they were making it clear that they were going to be playing strictly by the rule book: there was no question of mercy. And so, even though Odinma had managed to raise £16,000 out of the total owed, and we had paid this to the landlord as a down payment with the assurance that the balance would be paid as soon as the landlord confirmed the final amount due, the landlord's eye was on the £1million windfall that he stood to gain from the lease being made forfeit. He had already started the reading of the last rites before burial of Odinma's interest in the penthouse by submitting an application to the Land Registry for the legal title to Odinma's lease to be cancelled and removed from the public register.

It now became a sorry tale of "if onlys". If only the U.S. Big Boys had not started the trouble that led to Odinma's cashflow problems. If only Odinma had thought of re-mortgaging the penthouse to raise the money to pay the landlord what was due. If only the Tribunal had stuck to the original hearing date for the arbitration. If only I had known earlier about the six months time limit for relief from forfeiture. Of such regrets there were many thoughts but of solutions I could think of none. It was time to bow to superior expertise.

Araba Taylor was from Ghana. Her father had been a highly respected Judge of the Supreme Court in the post-independence administration. Having inherited the legal genes from him, she had obtained excellent honours in law from Cambridge University. We had been at Bar School together where I recall being slightly intimidated by the quality of her CV as compared to my own humble beginnings. She had at least made it into practice at the Chancery Bar although, with such pedigree, had she been one of the daughters of the soil she would have been a Queen's Counsel; but she was not.

I sent the papers across to her and not long afterwards she demonstrated her excellence. Having carefully tracked the confusing history of the Penthouse through some inter-company transfers, she had noted that the company that the landlord's solicitors had taken to be the landlord in relation to the Penthouse was not the landlord; it was only the management company. Thus we had a situation where the original claim, against Odinma's offshore company (as the owner of the 999 year Lease), had been issued by "Management Co. Ltd" in the mistaken belief that it was "Landlord Co. Ltd" and judgment had been obtained and enforced by the wrong legal entity which in fact had no right to the Judgment. On speaking with the Land Registry it turned out that they too had noted the discrepancy and had queried it. It turned out that the landlord's solicitors had through some weasel words in their explanation managed to persuade the Land Registry to treat as a technicality something that was in fact fundamental.

With a mixture of relief and glee, I wrote to bring the fortunate turn of events to the landlord's solicitor's attention. Now it was their turn to agonise over the "if onlys". The letter invited them to accept that the judgment they had obtained could not stand in the circumstances and proposed that they join in signing a consent order to set the judgment aside subject to Odinma paying the outstanding arrears of ground rent and service charges.

Having come so close to picking up a million pound windfall, the landlord was not about to roll over. We were going to have to persuade the court to set the original judgment aside. They would, in any event, be making an application for the court to allow the name of the Landlord Co. Ltd to be substituted for that of the Management Co, Ltd so that the judgment could stand.

This was the counter-attack strategy that their barrister, Michelle Stevens-Hoare of Hardwicke Chambers, had advised and she was in court to make the case. She had been called to the Bar in 1986, the year after my call. Hers was a style of advocacy that was mild in temperament but incisive in its effect. Always confident in her logic she was hard to ruffle – any serve was always returned. Her argument was a bold one. It was based on Rule 19.2 of the Civil Procedure. Rules which reads as follows:

> *19.2-(1) This rule applies where a party is to be added or substituted except where the case falls within rule 19.5 (special provisions about changing parties after the end of a relevant limitation period).*
>
> *(2) The court may order a person to be added as a new party If-*
>
> *(a) it is desirable to add the new party so that the court can resolve all the matters in dispute in the proceedings; or*
>
> *(b) there is an issue involving the new party and an existing party which is connected to the matters in dispute in the proceedings, and it is desirable to add the new party so that the court can resolve that issue.*
>
> *(3) The court may order any person to cease to be a party if it is not desirable for that person to be a party to the proceedings.*
>
> *(4) The court may order a new party to be substituted for an existing one if-*
>
> *(a) the existing party's interest or liability has passed to the new party; and*
>
> *(b) it is desirable to substitute the new party so that the court can resolve the matters in dispute in the proceedings.*

Not being able to show that Management Co. Ltd's "interest or liability" had passed to Landlord Co. Ltd so as to have the latter substituted for the former under Rule 19.2(4), Ms Stevens-Hoare was seeking to achieve the same result by using Rule 19.2(2)(a) to get Landlord Co. Ltd added as a party to the action that Management Co. Ltd. had commenced, and secured judgment in, without *locus standi*. Once that had been done, she was seeking to use Rule 19.2 (3), to get Management Co. Ltd to be released from the action.

For this dribble to have any chance of success, the landlord's application had to be dealt with by the Judge before the application that we had already made for the judgment that had been wrongfully obtained by the Management Co. Ltd to be set aside. By some behind the scenes manoeuverings the landlord's application was given a date ahead of our application even though we had filed our application first.

Odinma, still cash-strapped, couldn't put the funds together to instruct Araba to see her arguments through in court but, with my confidence in the outcome of the arbitration being as it was, I was ready to do the advocacy and to leave the fees on the slate.

To our shock and amazement, the District Judge proceeded to accept the landlord's case. He ruled: *"It seems to me that this is a matter where it is desirable for the new party to be added…it seems to me a case where there is no difference whatsoever other than really in the name of the parties"*. He went on to justify his decision by saying: *"It seems to me that if I refused the claimant's application that I would, in fact, be refusing it in circumstances that allowed the Defendants to seize an advantage rather than show prejudice in their own right"*.

I was amazed by the judge's sense of what was just whereby a landlord who was now owed no more than £4,000 was now to be handed a windfall of £1million and by the manner in which the outcome had been secured. It had involved our earlier-in-time application, which was bound to succeed, being pushed back behind a later application by the landlord and, further, the plain meaning of the legislation had been distorted. An even sorrier spectacle was to see Odinma, a powerfully built man, burst into tears in court. I consoled him by whispering to him that we would appeal the judgment.

As soon as it became apparent that the appeal was to be heard by Judge Brian Knight QC of the Central London Court, I was confident. I had appeared before him on an appeal once before and I knew him to be a judge who honoured the overriding objective of the Civil Procedure Rules, which was to hear cases "justly". And true to expectation, the first thing that Judge Knight did on the appeal was to issue a direction that Odinma's application to set aside the default judgment should be before the court at the same time as the landlord's application for Landlord Co., Ltd to be substituted for Management Co., Ltd so that all matters could be dealt with in one hearing. He then proceeded to deal with Odinma's application first as being the first in time and granted the application and allowed the appeal.

However, having been encouraged by the lower court's dubious judgment, the owner of Landlord Co., Ltd wasn't ready to give up just yet. He sought and was granted leave to appeal Judge Knight's judgment to the Court of Appeal. With a £1million prize in prospect, a stake of £20,000 on the legal costs of an appeal was worth it. At the very least it gave them a position to negotiate from. On our side we knew that we could not be certain of justice third time round. The waters having been thus muddied by the justice system, each side had an incentive to cut a deal.

A deal was done on terms that Odinma would get his penthouse back on payment of what was effectively a cash windfall of £100,000 to the landlord which would be paid as soon as Odinma got the money that he was expecting from the arbitration. Good business having been done by the businessmen, they shook hands and exchanged cards and left the lawyers to tie up the loose ends. In the end Odinma never did pay Araba for her advice that saved his Penthouse because, as it turned out, having taken his opponent's business card he ended up paying the settlement monies directly to him and behind our backs.

Justice Delayed

Meanwhile on the arbitration front, as both Odinma's company and my firm tottered on the edge of our credit lines and functioned at the mercy of our bankers, I was simply left to reflect on the adage : "Justice delayed is justice denied".

The case underlined how the bigger party in a litigation could ultimately frustrate justice simply by virtue of its extra staying power through its greater financial stamina. This case was especially perverse given that part of the financial muscle that the bigger party was standing on were substantial commissions that should properly have been paid over to the smaller party. In such circumstances interest and damages awarded to the smaller party may well be too little, too late.

Finally, for an arbitration that was first formally requested in June, 2003, and the three-day hearing of which finished on 17 September, 2004, we were informed by the Secretariat that the draft final Decision of the Tribunal had been submitted to the ICC on 31 August, 2005.

The Decision now had to be submitted for approval at the "next sitting" of the Court. If approved by the Court the decision would be sent to the parties by the Secretariat, if not it would be sent back to the Tribunal for re-consideration. On 29 September, 2005, the decision was finally approved by the Court. That the decision was unanimous in our favour was no surprise but the devil was in the detail.

It read more like an imposed settlement than a reasoned judgment on the issues as argued by the parties before the Tribunal. It failed to do justice to the quality of the blows that the pugilists had landed on each other. What should have been declared a TKO had been announced as a points victory albeit on a unanimous decision. From the first (and last) race discrimination case that I had argued before an Employment Tribunal, I had come to appreciate that a "unanimous decision" was often a compromise decision. In this case the compromise was patronising based on the belief that the small players would be content with half a loaf.

Justice Betrayed

Well at least the wait was over and, more importantly, we could now get paid. The rule on costs being the English rule that "loser pays", the U.S. Big Boys were liable to pay our fees in addition to the $3million-odd that the Tribunal had awarded to Odinma as commissions due.

Business runs best on trust but if any case illustrated the abuse of trust there was none more so than this Odinma matter. With hindsight it is possible to see that Odinma's battle with the U.S. Big Boys was nothing more than a dogfight in which neither side occupied any moral high ground because as soon as the hearing closed, Odinma had started scheming as to how he could avoid paying the success fee that he had pledged to us, as well as the fees on the penthouse instruction.

Anticipating that the compensation that the U.S. Big Boys were going to have to pay him would be paid into our account as his legal representatives, he had started sending us all sorts of irrevocable instructions addressed to us for sizeable sums that he claimed his bankers in Nigeria had got him to sign as a condition of extending his credit facilities. As far as I was concerned these bilateral agreements between him and his bankers could only bite to the extent of any money that was his. However, the agreements were never tested because, for some then unknown reason, the U.S. Big Boys gave notice that they would be making the payments directly into the accounts of Odinma's company in Nigeria, full details of which they had from all the financial records that Odinma had disclosed.

The reason for the American's move was not at the time clear but, he being our client, we were loathe to insist that the monies should be paid to us. Besides I was still confident that given all that had been done for him Odinma would honour the bargain in respect of the success bonus. However we had no qualms in insisting that our fees for the arbitration be paid directly to us.

It slowly dawned that just as those who place a premium on honour find it difficult to part with their good name, so those who place a premium on the accumulation of money find it difficult to part with it. Now that the money was under his control, Odinma was calling the shots. His attitude was that the fee that we had received from the U.S. Big Boys, based on our hourly rate, should suffice as compensation for the work we did. He was right, but in no way did it compensate for the risk that we took, nor for the two years that we had had to wait to be paid. First he quibbled whether he had ever agreed to pay a success bonus, then when the evidence was sent to him he sought to renegotiate the deal.

The decision in the arbitration had been an imposed settlement in that the Tribunal had turned a blind eye to the fact that the U.S. Big Boys had failed to make disclosure of documents that would have enabled us to calculate the true figure of net revenue and simply awarded him a figure that was a little over fifty percent of what he was claiming. My guess was that the figure that he was entitled to was in excess of $10million. I had identified two lines of attack. One was to appeal the decision on the very narrow ground that is permitted in arbitration cases. The other was to institute court proceedings in the U.S.. Before the stand off over the payment of our success fee started, I had started some crucial ground work in sketching out the plan of argument for round two and it was looking good. With his secret design in mind, Odinma had been urging me on to finish the case strategy for this round two and I had effectively finished by the time it became clear that he was playing on my trust just as the U.S. Big Boys had done to him.

His offer now was that he would pay $130,000 of the success fee now, if I could just wait until we had finished round two as he had so many debts to pay off. This was of course the very trick that the U.S. Big Boys had used on him that had given rise to the litigation in the first place. I told him that he hardly needed reminding that he would not have been in a position to pay any of these debts that had suddenly become a priority but for my efforts and that he was effectively asking me to fund round two from the unpaid success fee for round one.

Suddenly, the man who had been weeping in court and hanging on my every word launched a verbal tirade full of the choicest expletives: "I have just been to hell and back because of what these guys did to me and I am not f***ing going back because of you or anybody" he said. If I wasn't prepared to accept his terms he would find someone else to argue round two.

I regarded the threat as idle at the time because even though he had the outline of the case strategy for round two all the files were in my possession. In any case I could not see which advocate he could find that would have a detailed enough understanding of the issues that had been argued in round one. Whoever was going to argue round two would have to know exactly what issues had been argued and settled in round one, so as not to be accused of attempting to re-open the issues in the arbitration which was not permissible.

I was on a trade mission to Kenya when my office called to say that we had been served with notice of new proceedings against Odinma's company instituted by the U.S. Big Boys. I could hardly believe my ears given the profound ingratitude that Odinma had shown. It was as if the gods had been watching the turn of events.

The U.S. Big Boys were now on the offensive because round one was a case that they hadn't envisaged losing. They felt that they had been caught by a lucky punch and now, having analysed the Tribunal's decision, they were initiating round two to get their money back. The reason they had insisted on paying the $3 million compensation monies directly to Odinma's company account in Nigeria was now clear: in the expectation of victory in round two, they needed to be able to track the money; they knew that they would have been powerless to do this if the money had gone into our client account.

The U.S. Big Boys had, quite naturally, assumed that I would be representing Odinma in the new battle and had named me as his Counsel in the new Request for Arbitration that they had filed. They did not know how things had fallen apart in Camp Victory. Although Odinma had been sent a copy of the Request for Arbitration directly by the Tribunal he wasn't calling me for obvious reasons.

With my name on the official papers as his advocate I had no choice but to break the ice. I took his words of apology with a pinch of salt. He explained that because I had broken off contact he had had to instruct someone else to represent him but that he would really like to have me argue the case. My position was that provided I got my success fee for round one I was ready to discuss terms for round two. As I was due in Lagos the following week we agreed to meet. The wait in his reception was slightly longer than usual but eventually his secretary came to take me up to his office.

"Dele! How now my brother? You see what these American b***tards are trying to do to me"?

He called for his secretary to bring him his file for the U.S. Big Boy's new arbitration request. He wanted to show me why he could not afford to pay me more than $130,000 at this stage because the new lawyer he had engaged had insisted on a substantial upfront payment as a condition of taking the case. Then he produced the letter from the Nigerian chambers of one Fidelis Oditah QC, SAN acknowledging the receipt of a cheque for $250,000 as a down payment for the new arbitration between his company and the U.S. Big Boys.

The development was all the more remarkable since on speaking with Odinma it emerged that the U.S. Big Boy's were basing their new action on an interpretation of the Tribunal's written judgment in round one. Here now was one of the three-man judicial panel that delivered the judgment in round one effectively stepping down from the role of the impartial judge in a dispute and accepting to conduct the fight for one of the parties against the other in a dispute centered upon the meaning of the unanimous judgment that he and his fellow arbitrators had rendered. How the ICC gave Oditah clearance to act was one puzzle I could not get my head around.

I was shocked but did not show it. I told him that I would have no problems working with Oditah on round two; my mission was to collect the payment that was due to me for the preparatory work that I had done on the round two that we had been proposing to initiate before the relationship turned sour.

Having collected my money I decided to put the sorry saga far behind me marveling, as I left, on the influence of money on the human condition. ▨

12. CLOSING ARGUMENTS: IF ARSENE WENGER WERE A LAWYER

Highbury is the home of the Arsenal and number 50 Framfield Road, London N5, where my story in England began, was within three hundred metres of the old Arsenal ground. The Emirates, the new Arsenal stadium, is closer still.

I loved football but hated the Arsenal. The beautiful game and the club simply did not sit comfortably together under the leadership of Terry Neil and later, his midfield hardman, George Graham. Arsenal made the beautiful game boring but neither their manager nor their supporters cared. Winning was all that mattered and "1-0 to the Arsenal" became the club anthem.

An alleyway connected Framfield Road to the smaller two-up-two-down terraced houses on the square that was Whistler Street. This street with its rich cast of working-class characters was a reality version of the classic English TV soap opera Coronation Street. The households of Colin and Steven Hills, first cousins born in the same year, were typical. Their mothers, who were sisters, had two children each and lived little more than two doors away from each other. With such a sense of community front doors were always left open as the children lived an open-plan lifestyle.

There was always football to be played on Whistler Street to the frustration of those who were unlucky enough to own the end-of-terrace houses, on whose side walls we marked out our goals with white chalk "borrowed" from Drayton Park School. In fact there were so many boys of around the same age in our neighbourhood that we formed a Saturday league football team called Whistler Street Rovers. It had to be a Saturday league rather than the more popular Sunday league because the team's playmaker (yours truly) was the only one in the 'hood whose parents were making him observe the old religion by going to church each Sunday.

How things can change. That Arsenal F.C. would become the epitome of the beautiful game, the "second preference" team of all non-fundamentalists; and that the entrance to the new home of this theatre of the performing arts would be directly across the road from Whistler Street leads me to be confident that the natural beauty of law and the practice of litigation will be rediscovered in England.

The Arsenal revolution took a visionary with courage to bring it about. That man was an outsider, the Frenchman Arsene Wenger, the philosopher-king of the beautiful game. The game remained the same but he changed the way Arsenal played it. Change, of course, is never easy for it is far easier to leave things as they are especially when the faithful are not complaining. It takes a visionary to see greater possibilities than the status quo.

Wenger transformed the culture of the Gooners from a "winning is all that matters" to trying to win with style. By restoring the natural beauty of the game he not only won trophies, he also won new converts to the Arsenal faith. A critical plank of the revolution was to open the barricades to talent from wherever it could be found, from Belarus (Alexander Hleb) to Ivory Coast (Kolo Toure). No longer were positions reserved for the old school boys from the Arsenal Academy.

He also allowed the game to rediscover its soul which is first and foremost leisure and entertainment. The conservativism of "don't care how you play, just don't get beat", gave way to the new liberalism of winning by allowing the players to give expression to their imagination and talents on pitch even if it meant that the occasional dribble didn't work or the odd point was dropped.

What is more, he revolutionised the education and training manuals. Whereas, according to the manuals, a right back had always been someone with a good right foot who happened to be fast enough to stop opposing attackers, he changed it to an Emmanuel Eboue, a two-footed footballer who was just as comfortable playing on the right of midfield or filling in as a No. 10. Whereas the midfielder had been the player in the mould of a marathon runner who could run the circuit of the pitch from the first whistle to the last, the midfielder became an artist, a Picasso, who could paint a masterpiece with the subtle angles through which he could stroke the ball either to those ahead of him or behind him or, if care was not taken by the opponents, directly into their goal.

Even now, from my seat, in Row 20, Block 134, Upper Tier, at the Emirates Stadium, facing the old haunt at Whistler Street, the debate between the old faithful and the new converts like me over the old way and the Wenger way rages on. The old guard hark back to the Ray Palours who played with their hearts while we of the new testament make the case for those like Eboue who play with their heads.

But thanks to the Wenger vision everyone who loves football is a Gooner now at heart though some will never confess it. Law, of course, is not a game but there are many lessons that those responsible for legal education and practice in England and Wales can learn from the Arsenal. It was this thought that led me to deliver a talk at my *Alma Mater*, London Metropolitan University, that was titled "If Arsene Wenger were a Lawyer".

It was a very curious audience that showed up on the day. One or two came in their Arsenal jerseys but all were fascinated to hear what I had to say about the parallels between law and football and what the equivalent in legal practice would be to a Thierry Henry.

The law is a very broad field with many aspects and disciplines yet underpinned by a common skill. That football is a physical endeavour and law is a cerebral occupation should not obscure the fact that both are engagements requiring a capacity to learn, a commitment to lengthy training, enhanced thinking skills and good judgment. Consider for a moment the speed of thought, calculation and judgment that it takes to volley a ball that is coming at you at pace, at an angle, and to instantly re-direct the ball past a goal keeper standing guard over a goal eight ft high and 24 ft wide as Marco van Basten, the Dutch striker, famously, and fabulously, did.

Further just as it is the combination of a footballer's training with his natural ability that shapes how he plays the game, so it is the quality of the lawyer's legal education combined with his aptitude for legal reasoning that makes the lawyer. The important lesson here is that natural ability is more important than the fact that one has received tutelage at the best schools. That one has been fortunate to have schooled at the Arsenal Academy with the equipment and training facilities does not mean that you can play the game better than a Kolo Toure who grew up playing bare-footed as we did in Aiyede. The key to getting the best is to recognise and embrace talent however conventional or unconventional the route it has come through may be.

What then of the positional equivalents between lawyers and footballers? In football, defenders are those who are able to keep their eyes on the ball at all times. The best ones are those who are able to read the game and anticipate what is going to happen rather than simply relying on their ability to react to what is happening. In law these are the lawyers with great attention to detail and, more often than not, they have formidable memories for data recall. Theirs is not to be flamboyant (unless of course they are of the new Arsenal mould) but to be safe. You will typically find these lawyers in highly technical disciplines like tax, pensions, insurance and property law.

Attackers are typically those with dexterity of the feet and a quick eye for an opening in the opponent's guard. Having spotted an opening, however narrow, the best are ruthless in driving home the advantage. Nothing illustrates this better than Andrey Arsharvin's first goal for Arsenal in the match against Blackburn Rovers. In law these flair players, and instinctive killers, are typically to be found in advocacy and litigation. They spend as much time honing their techniques for the kill as they do studying their opposition to plan how they will open up his guard. A moment's hesitation by the opposing defenders is often all that the master predator needs for the fatal ambush. In the same way, a series of well-chosen questions can lead a defendant into a cul de sac from which there is no return.

Then there are the midfielders. These are the "total-footballers"; the true masters of their subject. They need to feel the ball more often than their team-mates in defence or attack. Their job is to form the first line of defence and the springboard of the attack and so they, above all, have to be multi-skilled. They must share enough of the defender's ability to anticipate danger and the striker's capacity to identify opportunities in order to draw the best out of their team-mates. Their equivalents in the world of law are the transactional lawyers or deal makers in the big law firms. The best can turn their hands to most areas of law but crucially they know when to pass the ball to their more specialized team mates and when to call for the pass back. One of the greats in this regard was Gordon Toland, the oldest partner in the tax department at Lovells at the time I joined.

He was a veritable City law firm in his own right: a superb legal mind. Heaven knows whether they have yet managed to persuade him to retire!

So then if Arsene Wenger were a lawyer, what would the law firm under his management look like? Would there be room in the team for the lawyer equivalents of the bare-footed Kolo Toures or would priority be given to those who had come through the Academy? Would the excellence of the advocate be made paramount above all else so as to win admiration even from neutrals or would preservation of the established order be all that mattered?

We will never know the answer but we can at least imagine. What we have for now is the established order. The Bar Council will tell you that they established a diversity team in 1992; that the Bar was the first profession to publish an equality and diversity code in 1995; that, moreover, compliance with the code is mandatory and is part of the Bar Code of Conduct. The Arsenal, before Arsene Wenger, had a similar commitment to equality of opportunity through which Paul Davis, Michael Thomas, and my Highbury Grove school-mate, Chris Whyte, took it in turns to be the exception that proved the rule. The establishment preferred to hold to the myth that if there weren't enough ethnic minority players making it through into the team it was simply because they were not good enough.

And Here The Case Rests

So, all said and done, Master Akindele Ogunetimoju never did quite make it to the English Bar. Having been called but not chosen, he had simply gate-crashed the party as a self-taught litigator and advocate. Despite his exploits in the million-dollar case the rules still said he had no right to appear in the higher courts of England until his competency as an advocate had been formally assessed. The assessment took the form of a ten-minute mock cross-examination of a mock witness (a hired actress) before a mock judge (a junior barrister). At the end of the exercise he was issued with a certificate which confirmed him as a solicitor-advocate with rights of audience in the courts of England. As to how he got on there, that story is next. ▨

END NOTES

1. On 28 April, 2009, *the Times* contained a law report from the Court of Appeal, Criminal Division, in which Claude Clifford Greaves was refused leave to appeal against his conviction at Southwark Crown Court, on his plea of guilty to three counts of false accounting, contrary to section 17 of the Theft Act 1968 and one count of aiding and abetting fraudulent trading, contrary to section 458 of the Companies Act 1985, for which he was imprisoned for concurrent terms of three years.

2. On 12 February, 2009 *Financial Times* reported that Kellogg, Brown & Root, the engineering, construction and services company (not the U.S. Big Boys!), and its former parent, Halliburton, had agreed to pay a combined $579m to settle U.S. criminal and civil allegations that KBR bribed Nigerian government officials to obtain contracts. This followed a report in *The Times* on 12 September, 2008, that Jeffrey Tesler, a suburban solicitor "who is based at a shabby office in Tottenham, North London, is accused of being a middleman for the payment of bribes to Nigerian officials between 1995 and 2004" from an international consortium awarded contracts to build a $6 billion (£3.5 billion) gas-production plant in Nigeria. According to the report, the consortium included the engineering consultancy M.W. Kellogg which was "taken over by the American company Halliburton, which was controlled by Dick Cheney until he became U.S. Vice-President in 2000". The report went on to state that "The British Government has admitted underwriting a £122 million loan for the project, now at the centre of one of the biggest bribery scandals."

Best Speaker

AWARD

presented to

DELE   OGUN

EARLY B:RD SPEAKER
Toastmasters Club

ROGER HARDING   25/06/09
President   Date

TOASTMASTERS INTERNATIONAL

601BS